Best wishes to Jane and Art,
two great friends for whom
I have the greatest respect
and admiration

Sincerely

D.A. "Andy" Anderson, author

Oct. 13, 1979

ALL THE
TREES AND WOODY PLANTS
OF THE BIBLE

A Tree Speaks

Ye who would pass by and raise your
hand against me, harken ere you harm
me. I am the heat of your hearth on the
cold winter nights, the friendly shade
screening you from the summer sun;
and my fruits are refreshing draughts
quenching your thirst as you journey
on. I am the beam that holds your house,
the board of your table, the bed on which
you lie, and the timber that builds your
boat. I am the handle of your hoe, the
door of your homestead, the wood of
your cradle, and the shell of your coffin. I am the gift of God and friend of
man. Ye who pass by, listen to my prayer.
Harm me not. I am a Tree.

—Anonymous, translated from Spanish.

ALL THE
TREES AND WOODY PLANTS
OF THE BIBLE

David A. Anderson

WORD BOOKS
PUBLISHER

Contents ⚜⚜⚜⚜⚜⚜⚜⚜⚜⚜⚜⚜

6. Biblical References to Trees and Woody Plants of the Bible 74

Preface

Educated as a forester and range manager in the biological sciences, I have had, and continue to have, an avid interest in plants mentioned or referred to in the Bible. This interest caused me to seek information, particularly of the trees and woody plants, from various historical sources. In so doing I hoped to gain a better understanding of the scriptural passages dealing with this vegetation.

Many questions have arisen: What was gopher wood from which Noah built his ark? How big, in everyday language, was the ark? What were the sources of frankincense and myrrh, the substances which were presented to Christ at his birth? Is there a difference between the almug tree and the algum tree which are referred to in two almost identical biblical passages? Did the "balm of Gilead" tree grow naturally in Bible lands? How did Amos "dress" the sycamore? Was there a "manna" tree? Were carob pods eaten only by animals? What were the tools of the forest workers and carpenters? To what extent were trees worshiped? What trees and other plants are referred to by indirect references? These and many other questions about trees and woody plants are encountered as one reads through the Bible.

Of additional interest was man's early and continuous use of many tree products mentioned in the Scriptures. Many, such as olive oil, charcoal, spices, tannin and others, played a significant role in everyday life. Wood also played an important role in shipbuilding, as a means of transportation, and for general construction and other purposes. To what extent were these products used? How extensive was the shipping industry? What did man make from wood in Bible times?

In parts of the Mediterranean world represented today by such countries as Italy, Greece, and Turkey, there were extensive commercial forest areas in biblical times. However, the holy lands, as we presently recognize them, were never extensively forested. Yet, from the pages of the Bible it is evident that forests, trees, and woody plants were formerly more widespread than they are today. The once abundant forests, represented by the cedars of Lebanon, no longer exist. How extensive were the original forest and tree areas of the holy lands? What social changes brought about the devastation of the trees and woody plants?

This book is a compendium of knowledge about biblical trees and woody plants, their usage, and other general information as compiled by the author over many years. It is not a technical presentation, but is rather a popular introduction to the subject for lay readers of the Bible. The narrative has been kept to a minimum, allowing the photographs and other illustrations to tell their story. It is a book in which the author desires to share his knowledge about plants of the Bible in the hope that it may increase the interest and pleasure of those who read the greatest Book of all. For a greater depth of study the reader's attention is called to the more exhaustive and technical references given at the close of the book and to the various versions of the Bible.

Many scriptural references are given in the text for the reader's benefit. Unless otherwise indicated, the King James Version is used.

DAVID A. ANDERSON

College Station, Texas

Acknowledgments

The author received aid or suggestions from a number of individuals and a variety of sources. To each he is indebted.

He is especially grateful to the following who provided either maps, pictures, resource references, aerial or space photography, publications, or helpful comments: R. T. Allen, Jr., Deputy Director, Basic and Geographic Intelligence, Central Intelligence Agency, Washington, D.C.; Mete Basci, Agriculture Attache, Turkish Embassy, Washington, D.C.; Robert A. Carlisle, Office of Information, Department of the Navy, Washington, D.C.; Cecil M. Carson, Corpus Christi, Texas; Gideon Cohen, Agricultural Attache, Embassy of Israel, Washington, D.C.; Creation Science Research Center, San Diego, California; Embassy of Syria, Washington, D.C.; Clayton D. Forbes, Team Leader, Agriculture, Range and Forestry, National Aeronautics and Space Administration, Houston, Texas; Jo Fessler, National Aeronautics and Space Administration, Washington, D.C.; Food and Agriculture Organization of the United Nations; Gordon Gay, College Station, Texas; Hal Harris, photographer, Bryan, Texas; William T. Hartman, Walnut Creek, California; Holy Ground Mission, Palestine, Texas; Walter E. Jeske, Chief, Education and Publications Branch, Soil Conservation Service, U.S. Department of Agriculture, Washington, D.C.; George M. Kyle, Bureau of Outdoor Recreation, U.S. Department of Interior, Washington, D.C.; Ralene Levy, Information Officer, Consulate

General of Israel in New York; Dr. N. Lipschitz, Head, Department of Botany, Tel Aviv University, Tel Aviv, Israel; Ruth Price, Photographic Division, U.S. Department of Agriculture, Office of Communications, Washington, D.C.; Barbara Raines, College Station, Texas; Richard W. Stephenson, Head, Reference and Bibliography Section, The Library of Congress; Washington, D.C.; Olin E. Teague, Congressman, Washington, D.C.; U.S. Forest Service, U.S. Department of Agriculture, Washington, D.C.; Y. Waisel, Department of Botany, Tel Aviv University, Tel Aviv, Israel; and Ralph W. Woolner, Information Officer, Department of Environmental Management, The Commonwealth of Massachusetts, Boston, Massachusetts.

The author is particularly indebted to the Reverend John W. Leonard, Jr., Minister, Church of Christ, Santa Fe, New Mexico, and to the Reverend H. Bailey Stone, Minister, First Baptist Church, Odessa, Texas, for their review and critique of the manuscript.

Lastly, he is indebted to his late mother and father, Margaret and Samuel Anderson, who nurtured and sustained in him a faith in God and a belief in the Holy Bible as the guide to faith and practice.

Uncredited photos and maps were supplied by the author. To avoid unnecessary repetition in captions, the following legend explains the abbreviations within the captions. The photos were supplied courtesy of:

Cecil M. Carson—CMC
Central Intelligence Agency—CIA
Consulate General of Israel in New York—CGI
Gordon Gay—GG
National Aeronautics and Space Administration—NASA
Simcha Levyadum, Tel Aviv University—SL
Soil Conservation Service—SCS
Texas Forest Service—TFS
B.P. Srivastava and Indian Forest Research Institute—BPS
United States Department of Agriculture—USDA
United States Forest Service—USFS

ALL THE
TREES AND WOODY PLANTS
OF THE BIBLE

Fig. 1–1. The beautiful flowering plant, Apple of Sodom, *Calotropis procera*, growing at Ein Gedi in Israel. No doubt Moses was familiar with it. While the Bible refers to many flowering plants, there are more references to trees and woody plants within its pages. SL

🍁 The Bible: An Anthology of Trees

THE MEN WHO WROTE THE BIBLE were individuals of many vocations: doctors, prophets, kings, priests, historians, and lawgivers. Yet, they spoke a common language when they lauded the wonders of creation. The starry skies, mountains, vales and other manifestations of nature were praised. Trees and other plants, including flowers, received special attention from them (*Fig. 1–1*). Greater importance was given to trees than to flowers, however, since they are more frequently mentioned.

As men of the soil, the biblical writers were familiar with trees, the grass their herds fed upon, and the habits of birds, insects, plants, and animals as they helped or hindered their efforts to secure a livelihood. The passage of birds on migration did not escape their attention, nor did other facets of nature, all of which are reflected in biblical passages.

15

Hundreds of references to trees and woody plants appear in the pages of the Bible. These references commence in the first chapter of Genesis with their creation and end in the last chapter of Revelation with the Tree of Life. As the psalmist said, trees were made for the glory of God (Ps. 148:9).

The Bible is an anthology of plants, and the Song of Solomon is the greatest plant catalog of the Scriptures.

While the cedars of Lebanon are referred to frequently, all trees, large or small, were a "tree of the Lord" *(Fig. 1–2)* and played an important role in the life of the people in biblical lands. Scriptural passages relate to the benefit of trees and to the destruction of trees. Some passages directly, or by simile or allegory, refer to forest fires and the disastrous effects of forest devastation.

To the Hebrews, fruit trees were espècially important since they provided food. Fruit trees were to be spared from the ravages of war. Only ordinary trees were to be cut down for use in warfare (Deut. 20:20).

Trees are used symbolically in the Bible to illustrate wisdom (Prov. 3:18), a good man (Ps. 1:3), and useless persons (Isa. 56:3). Similarly, an olive tree with grafted stock is used to relate to the Gentiles who believed in God (Rom. 11:24).

Trees are also used in parables in both the Old and New Testaments, as well as in allegories (Judg. 9:7–15; 2 Kings 14:9; Mark 4:26–29; Luke 13:6–9). This indicates the important role of trees in the life of the people who lived close to the land.

Easily overlooked in biblical reading is the fact that one of the plagues of Egypt caused the vessels or cells of wood in all trees to become bloody. The Lord commanded Moses: "Say unto Aaron, Take thy rod, and stretch out thine hand upon the waters of Egypt, upon their streams, upon their rivers, and upon their ponds, and upon their pools of water, that they may become blood; and there may be blood throughout all the land of Egypt, both in wood and in stone" (Exod. 7:19).

Fig. 1–2. Trees were made for the glory of God and for man's use and enjoyment. TFS

Perhaps the most noteworthy trees of the Bible were the Tree of Life and the Tree of Knowledge. These were trees placed by God in the garden as related in the Genesis account of creation. Some biblical scholars consider these trees merely symbolic or spiritual. To most others, they were real.

God endowed Adam with everything required for the development of his nature and the fulfillment of his destiny in the garden of trees. From the fruit trees of the garden Adam would obtain his sustenance. In the Tree of Life he would find preservation from death. The Tree of Knowledge would provide training for his moral character, while the care of the garden would give him physical strength. Additionally, his concern with the vegetable and animal kingdoms would develop his intellect.

The Tree of Life and the Tree of Knowledge were fruit trees, but the nature of the fruit is unknown. The Tree of Knowledge was used as an instrument by God to test the obedience of Adam and Eve. Probably its fruit was unlike that of other trees in the garden. The sin was in the eating of that which God had forbidden. It was a rebellion against God's rule. For this, Adam and Eve were driven out of the Garden of Eden by God.

The Tree of Life was also a special tree in the midst or central portion of the garden. It appears in Revelation as a fruit-bearing tree with healing leaves (Rev. 22:2).

An ancient Babylonian inscription states: "Near Eridu was a garden in which was a mysterious Sacred Tree, a Tree of Life, planted by the gods, whose roots were deep, while its branches reached to heaven, protected by guardian spirits, and no man enters."

Eridu is the traditional site of the Garden of Eden. It is located about twelve miles south of biblical Ur, the home of Abraham.

A Tree of Life is symbolically found in the history of many religions. In Egypt, it was pictured as a large sycamore upon which the gods sit and obtain immortality from eating. The mythology of India describes it as a tree in

Fig. 1–3. These veteran olive trees are located in what is believed to be the Garden of Gethsemane where Christ went for meditation and prayer.

heaven from which Yama and other gods partake of the life-giving drink, "soma."

It was to a garden of trees, the Garden of Gethsemane, *(Fig. 1–3)*, that Christ went for meditation and prayer (Matt. 23:36; John 18:1, 2).

Truly, trees have been closely associated with man throughout the ages. This is reflected in hundreds of biblical passages. What sermons trees and forests could preach to the one who has ears to hear! (Job 12:8).

In the chapters that follow, the text is primarily restricted to a summary discussion of biblical trees and woody plants and the role these plants played in the life of the people in this period. While the Bible was the principal source of the material presented, other historical and archeological reports were used as a basis of information.

2

✹ Man's Relationship to the Environment

FROM GENESIS TO REVELATION the pages of the Bible reveal man's progress throughout the ages and his relationship to the universe in which he lived. Records of past civilizations left by man, and subsequent history, add to this knowledge.

When the people of antiquity first stalked the earth in search of food, clothing, and shelter, the basic necessities of life, they were surrounded by many mysterious forces and laws of nature. Man questioned these mysteries so as to better understand them, and in the process of solving one mystery at a time, gradually added to his knowledge.

He became curious as to the movement of the stars, the ebb and flow of the tides, seasonal winds, earthquakes, volcanoes, rocks of varied color, and the nature of trees and other plants. He viewed with awe these and many other facets of nature.

Neither can we dismiss his curiosity about the fire with which he cooked his food and the fuels he used for this purpose. Various trees and plants held a fascination for him and he subsequently learned how they could provide his many needs for food, clothing, shelter, and medication.

When early man could not understand things in nature, to them he paid homage, worshiping them as gods. Lacking an understanding of the true God, his fear and puzzlement caused him to create many mythical divinities in his own image. He endowed them with divine power over nature that he did not have. Then by honoring these gods with temples and sacrifices, he called upon them to remove his fears and help him achieve his goals in life *(Fig. 2–1)*. Trees are among the mythical divinities he accepted as having divine power. The Bible refers to this tree worship by the pagans. Such trees, however, have long since died. They do not remain today as evidence, as do the temples.

The Athenians had many gods among which was the "unknown God" *(Fig. 2–2)* of which Paul spoke (Acts 17:22, 23).

Early Egyptians worshiped a god known by the names of Osiris, Tammuz, Attis, and Adonis, symbolizing the yearly decay and revival of vegetable life. There were other man-made tree gods to which man turned.

As man progressed to the point where he was not so busy with the problems of mere survival, he had time for concentrated thought. It was then that he sought solace in high mountains, in forests, or under large trees to consider himself. Why was he born? What was his purpose in life? What follows death? What was his relation to nature? The prophets of the Bible afforded inspired answers to such questions (2 Peter 1:20, 21).

Eventually, through accumulated knowledge, he set forth to conquer nature as his abilities would permit. For a short period in history he succeeded *(Fig. 2–3)*.

Former civilizations uncovered in the sands of the deserts of biblical lands attest to the ambitions of men who built great cities, only to see them fall *(Fig. 2–4)*. Areas

Fig. 2–1. The well-known Parthenon on the Acropolis of Athens. Within the temple, the man-made goddess Athena, the goddess of wisdom, was worshiped. She was one of many gods created by man to whom he paid homage. The tree gods man worshiped at this time do not stand as a memorial today.

Fig. 2–2. Adjacent to the Acropolis in Athens stands Mars Hill, in foreground. It was from this hill that Paul spoke to the Athenians about the "unknown God"; this God was not a spirit in a tree or made of stone by man.

Fig. 2–3. At its zenith, Mesopotamia was a fertile valley supporting 40 million people. A land of rich fields watered by an intricate system of canals, it was a powerful, inventive, and boastful nation. Yet the people failed, with all their knowledge, to see their dependence on nature. Overgrazing and denudation of the adjacent hills of trees induced extensive erosion; as a result, the canals clogged with silt. People fled the land and it became a desolation (sketch courtesy Gene Coulter and the Wyoming Game and Fish Commission).

Fig. 2–4. The ruins of Kish, one of the world's most important cities of over 5,000 years ago. It was excavated from the desert sands by archeologists in 1936. Kish was the first capital after the great flood that swept over Mesopotamia. It was located along the Euphrates River, south of Babylon. SCS

which formerly were lush with grass and trees are now wastelands. The people of antiquity who made the deserts bloom through irrigation saw the desert return to swallow them up.

In later years, at the time of Christ, it was the Roman Empire which ruled for five centuries. The Romans were, perhaps, the world's most exhaustive exploiters of both man and the natural resources *(Fig. 2–5)*. And one cannot overlook the exhaustive exploitation by the Arabs and the Turks who ruled over the Holy Land following the Romans.

While wars contributed to the decline of some civilizations, it was man's gross misunderstanding of nature that contributed in a large measure to his own downfall. Wanton destruction of the forests which led to soil erosion is but one example. Forgetting the lessons learned from his forebears about man's relationship to the environment, he failed to fall back on the experience of others of the past.

Yet, as man's knowledge increased over the centuries he rose to ever increasing heights. These advanced civilizations failed for the same reason. Man did not wish to accept the fact that he was but a steward of the land. Rather, he approached nature as an adversary only to invite his own destruction. He was determined to control nature on this planet we call earth. The result was inevitable. Man deluded himself into thinking he was getting something for nothing.

Even today these forces are at work. Will man learn to respect nature and work with it? Experiences of the past should teach us that we must adapt. Some have learned this lesson while others have not.

God, who made man from the dust, established natural laws in harmony with moral laws. One who would gain most must first know the natural laws and work as harmoniously as possible with them.

Man is but a part of the scheme of the environment. God

Fig. 2–5. During the Roman Empire, the vast forests in part of the Mediterranean Sea area were wantonly exploited. This scene in biblical Macedonia, now part of Yugoslavia, is evidence. After centuries, the once dense forests have not returned to their former productivity.

did not make him to destroy, but rather to use wisely the natural resources he provided and to enjoy the beauty of the earth.

Trees and other green plants are part of the intricate interrelationship which we call nature. Using energy from the sun, they combine it with water and carbon dioxide to produce food. In this process the plants liberate oxygen into the atmosphere for use by animal life, including man. It is this chlorophyll cycle on which man is totally dependent.

Man has been neglectful, or intolerant, of the role of trees and other green plants in the cycle of life. However, there are evidences of an effort to renew a working partnership with nature. This can only come about by using the resources wisely, restoring lands to their greatest productivity, and protecting them. "Then shall all the trees of the wood rejoice" (Ps. 96:12; 1 Chron. 16:33).

3

✹ Tree Areas
of
Bible Lands

Trees in the Geologic Past

There is little evidence to indicate what trees and other woody plants were indigenous to Bible lands during the various geologic periods or epochs *(Fig. 3–1)*. It is known that, in the geological past, the Palestine-Syrian area was separated from the north by a wide arm of the Mediterranean Sea which cut deeply into Asia. Eventually, when the Mediterranean sea lost this eastern branch, and an open land connection was established, it permitted trees and other plants to migrate slowly southward into the holy lands.

Scientists say that during the Miocene epoch the Mediterranean Sea became dry. It filled up again during the Pliocene epoch *(Fig. 3–1)* and has remained a deep body of water since then. In its dryness, the former sea became a hot desert basin 10,000 feet below sea level. This

Era	Period	Epoch	CHARACTERISTIC LIFE
Cenozic (Recent Life)	QUATERNARY 1½-2*	RECENT PLEISTOCENE 1½-2*	
	TERTIARY 65	PLIOCENE 7 MIOCENE 26 OLIGOCENE 37-38 EOCENE 53-54 PALEOCENE 64-65	
Mesozoic (Middle Life)	CRETACEOUS 136 JURASSIC 190-195 TRIASSIC 225		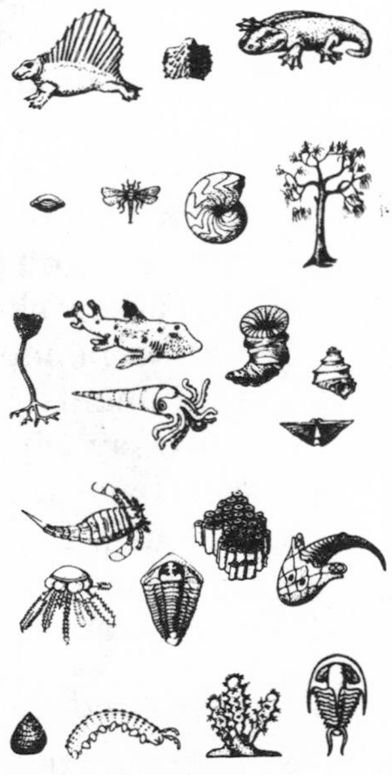
Paleozoic (Ancient Life)	PERMIAN 280 PENNSYLVANIAN 345 MISSISSIPPIAN 345 DEVONIAN 395 SILURIAN 430-440 ORDOVICIAN 500 CAMBRIAN 570	CARBONIFEROUS PERIOD	
Precambrian	3000-3400		

*Age of base in millions of years
Geologists estimate age of earth at 3,300,000,000 years

Fig. 3–1. Geologic time chart as developed by geologists. It is based on the type of ancient fossil plants and animals that have been preserved in the rocks of the earth's crust (Characteristic Life courtesy Bureau of Economic Geology, the University of Texas).

condition obviously had an effect on the vegetation throughout the Mediterranean region, and only the most arid woody plants could have survived such extreme climatic conditions in this period before recorded history.

It is speculated that, with the resubmergence of the Mediterranean Sea, subsidence of the basin and an uplift of surrounding lands took place.

According to scientists, vegetation of the Bible area has not changed appreciably since the Pleistocene geologic epoch *(Fig. 3-1)*, being subject only to minor climatic oscillations.

Today the evaporation loss from the Mediterranean Sea is about 1000 cubic miles. Only a tenth of this loss is compensated by rainfall and by the influx of fresh water from rivers. To maintain its level, water comes from the Atlantic Ocean through the Strait of Gibraltar. Yet, this sea, with such moisture as it provides, exerts an influence on vegetation which grows in parts of the Bible lands. The olive tree is an example. It never thrives far from the sea since mists are required for its growth. Nor does it generally grow in elevations above 2000 feet. The former cedars of Lebanon also depended on the sea for some of their moisture requirements.

To say what tree species grew in Bible lands millions of years ago would be conjecture. Yet, it is known that pine did grow in part of the area at some period in history, since the fossil resin amber was known in biblical times. This is discussed in Chapter 6.

Trees and the Universal Flood

About 5000 years ago Noah's ark rested on the mountains of Ararat, following the 150-day flood which encompassed the earth (Gen. 8:4, 11). Obviously, a flood of this magnitude would have an adverse effect on the trees and other woody vegetation then existing upon the earth, including the Bible lands. The biblical account deals with it as a world disaster in which the entire human race, except

Fig. 3–2. A Bristlecone pine *(Pinus aristata)*, growing in the Inyo National Forest of California, is the
oldest living thing on the face of the earth. Shown is a
tree in the Patriarch Grove at 11,000 feet elevation,
growing on a shallow dolomite soil in a harsh environment of snow, ice, and wind. USFS, USDA

Noah and his family, were wiped out. It resulted in the destruction of many animals and plants in every portion of the earth, and involved forces of nature on a scale unparalleled in the history of our planet earth (Gen. 7:11). Surprisingly, an event similar to it is recorded in the accounts of 40 out of over 53 mythologies.

While there are those who doubt the biblical account of the universal flood, notwithstanding that it has been reported in many diverse ancient cultures throughout the world, it is of interest to note that there is no record today of any tree exceeding 5000 years of age upon the earth. Age is determined by counting the annual rings of a tree. The life span of a tree varies, of course, by species. The gray birch is old at 40 years. Some oaks live as long as 2000 years, and the giant sequoias are about 4000 years of age. A few tree species have been reported to exceed 4000 years. However, the oldest living plant is a bristlecone pine *(Figs. 3–2 and 3–3)*, estimated by scientists to be 4600 years old. It is located in the White Mountain District of the Inyo National Forest in California.

Job referred to the universal flood when he stated: "Hast thou marked the old way which wicked men have trodden, which were cut down out of time, whose foundation was overflown with a flood?" (Job 22:15, 16). Many biblical records, other than the Genesis account, refer to the universal flood (Isa. 54:9; Luke 3:36; Matt. 24:37, 38; Heb. 11:7; 1 Peter 3:20; and 2 Peter 2:5).

With a universal flood of such duration, the question arises as to how any plant was able to survive. Obviously, trees and other plant life kept under water 150 or more days would naturally die from lack of air. Yet, it is recorded that an olive tree survived (Gen. 8:11). A dove plucked a leaf from an olive tree and brought it to Noah in the ark, indicating to him that the "waters were abated from off the earth."

From the biblical account it is unlikely that seeds of various tree and shrub species were taken by Noah into the

Fig. 3–3. This dead Bristlecone pine, sculptured by wind, sand, and ice, is, in its grotesqueness, a thing of beauty. With old limbs outstretched to the heavens, it is as a suppliant. USFS, USDA

ark. One must assume that, through God's providence, various forms of plant life survived the flood to gradually reestablish themselves and spread upon the earth.

If, as some have speculated, the flood commenced in November of our present calendar, this would be the season, as least on part of our earth with present climatological conditions, when trees are producing fruit. Yet, trees could have been producing fruit under other climatological conditions. These fruits and seeds could float upon the water and germinate following the recession of the flood waters. Some tree seed with heavy seed coats could have remained in place or floated upon the water and germinated later following the 150-day submergence period. Other tree seed could have been carried aloft by the wind, only to fall and germinate later. Additionally, it can be speculated that various species of uprooted trees and broken twigs of trees could have floated on the water, survived the flood, and reestablished themselves. Willow and cottonwood are but two of many trees that can readily establish themselves by asexual means. The olive can be reproduced in this manner too.

Some religious authorities hold the view that prior to the flood there was a greater variety of plants, including trees, and that the species still in existence were then much larger and more widely distributed over the face of the earth. They cite, as one example of distribution, that such trees as sequoia, walnut, and oak were at one time growing in the polar regions.

While there is no evidence to connect the tradition of the Day of the Dead to the universal flood, it is significant, as some have speculated, that this world-wide event, in all ancient, heathen, and present-day cultures, was connected with the memory of the dead or was observed as a feast to the ancestors. Of interest is the fact that the event occurs during the same calendar period. Usually it was observed at the disappearance of Pleiades, at the end of October or beginning of November.

The Druids, which kept a sacred fire burning all year, extinguished the fire around November 1. Additionally, all other fires were to be extinguished on this sacred date. It was believed that in darkness throughout the land, the spirits of those who died during the preceding year were carried to the judgment seat of the god of the dead.

The former bonfires of the Scotch and Welsh and the torches of the Irish on All Saints and All Souls Days, a strange relic of the festival of the Druids, is represented in our Halloween (Hallow Eve).

There is also the question as to climatological conditions before and after the flood. Naturally, a change in climate would influence the tree-vegetation pattern throughout the earth. Some authorities point to biblical evidence to indicate there was a change. They say the preflood earth had no rain as such, with the moisture requirements for trees and other green plants being dependent upon dew. Dew in turn was dependent upon humidity, saturation, temperature, dewpoint, and condensation. The basis for this assumption is found in Genesis 1:67 and Genesis 2:5, 6. It is also stated by these authorities that the temperatures were tropical and mild from pole to pole. There were no air-mass circulations. One conjecture is that the earth changed its axis and brought about the conditions which exist today.

Without alluding to a flood, some scientists are of the opinion that the earth may have turned on its axis during the geological past.

Some biblical authorities point out that, following the flood, man, animal, and plant life first became acquainted with cold weather, winds, storms, and desert and tropical heat. The earth was no longer a paradise of the original creation. The basis for this belief is Genesis 8:22 which states, "While the earth remaineth, seedtime and harvest, and cold and heat, and summer and winter, and day and night shall not cease" (Fig. 3–4).

It is of biological interest that God first caused the rainbow to be noted among clouds after the flood. It was a

Fig. 3–4. Did our earth tilt on its axis sometime in the geologic past? Following the flood the Lord said to Noah: "While the earth remaineth, seedtime and harvest, and cold and heat, and summer and winter, and day and night shall not cease." Some authorities speculate that, on the basis of this statement, our earth tilted on its axis at the time of the flood. NASA

covenant between God and Noah and his heirs (Gen. 9:9–17). And God said, "This is the token of the covenant which I make between me and you and every living creature that is with you, for perpetual generations" (Gen. 9:12). The rainbow would tend to prove that God, in his infinite wisdom, did cause a change in the atmosphere of our earth. It implies that trees and other plants would, henceforth, have to adapt to a changed climate.

There are also those who point to cataclysmic change on and within the earth's surface during the flood. They refer to evidences of humid, warm temperatures, or at least temperate forest climates, in the polar regions based on fossil broadleaf hardwoods found in these locations *(Fig. 3–5)*. Geologic discoveries show that desert areas such as the Sahara, the Great Australian Desert, the Chilean Ata-

Fig. 3–5. A fossil Glossopteris leaf associated with coal deposits from the glossopterid forests of the Permian age in the Ellsworth Mountains of Antarctica (photo courtesy D. L. Schmidt, U.S. Geological Survey).

Fig. 3–6. Portions of large petrified trees which once grew in Sandoval County, New Mexico. These occurred in the red sandstone and shale formation overlying the coal beds in the Hagen coal field (photo courtesy W. T. Lee, U.S. Geological Survey).

cama and the arid regions of the American West were at one time well-watered, swampy and humid, and supported the growth of trees *(Fig. 3–6)*.

The petrified forests of the western United States do contain broadleaf, deciduous trees, coniferous species and palms. In Yellowstone National Park, fossils of many trees have been found, among which are hickory, laurel, sycamore, persimmon, and ash. Other parts of the earth also contain fossilized trees not indigenous to the area today.

In Upper Cretaceous coals *(Fig. 3–1)*, such fossil plants as sassafras, laurel, tulip trees, magnolia, cinnamon, sequoia, poplar, willow, maple, birch, chestnut, elder, beech, elm, and palms have been found. In the Tertiary formation *(Fig. 3–1)* in England and the Continent fossilized remains of fig, cinnamon, palm, cypress, sequoia, magnolia, oak, plum, almond, myrtle, and acacia have been reported, some genera of which are found only in the United States today.

Many geologists do not subscribe to the universal flood as one that created the geological conditions existing today. To them, fossils have become increasingly important as a means of determining the age of the earth's structure *(Fig. 3–1)*. They consider the flood as an impractical theory.

According to geologists, trees do not represent the oldest type of life forms in the history of the vegetable kingdom. Rather, they say, they are fairly modern in the geological scale.

In the earliest development of the world's past, for which organic remains exist, the geologists tell us that the vegetable kingdom was represented by aquatic or semi-aquatic plants.

They say that, in succeeding geological ages, land plants "developed." In the period represented by our coal resources (Carboniferous period—*Fig. 3–1*) and the epoch preceding it, the earth became clothed with vegetation such as ferns, the ginkgo trees, *(Fig. 3–7)* and other minor plants. Later, in subsequent geologic periods, more land tree species "developed."

There are some religious leaders who believe the earth was inhabited by angels prior to the creation of man. They base their belief on such passages of Scripture as 2 Peter

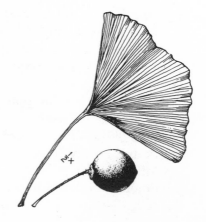

Fig. 3–7. Fan-shaped ginkgo leaf and fruit. Ginkgo is a living fossil native to China. It is related to the conifers. Geologists say it was one of the first trees to inhabit the earth in the geologic past. USFS, USDA

2:4–6; 1 John 3:4; Isaiah 14:12; Ezekiel 28:14–17; and Psalm 104:30. The angels sinned in the transgression of God's law. As a result, physical disaster came to the earth. The earth became "without form and void" (Gen. 1:2) or, in other words, in confusion and chaos, waste and empty. Then, in six days God renewed the face of the earth (Ps. 104:30) and created man. The angels were disqualified from developing and improving upon the universe, including earth, because they failed to improve and develop it when the opportunity was given to them. Assuming trees and other plants were present during the habitation of the angels as conjectured, it is obvious they also would have been destroyed and may be numbered among the tree fossils found today.

While man may speculate as to what trees and woody plants grew where and when in any period of the earth's history, only God knows the right answer. The answer is aptly given in his sublime message to Job when the Lord answered him out of a whirlwind and said, "Where wast thou when I laid the foundations of the earth? declare, if thou hast understanding" (Job 38:4).

Truly, the decrees of God are his eternal purposes.

Biblical and Historical Records of Tree Areas

As we look at Bible lands today, one wonders about the forests, trees, and other woody vegetation present throughout this region, and particularly the Fertile Crescent (Fig. 3–8), the cradle of civilization, about the time of Moses.

Especially does one ponder about such vegetation which once graced the highland mountains, slopes, and stream bottoms of the "Promised Land," helping to make it one of "milk and honey."

While the holy lands, overall, were mostly arid and never a forested region, as judged by the mean annual rainfall (Fig. 3–9), they were more tree-covered at the time of

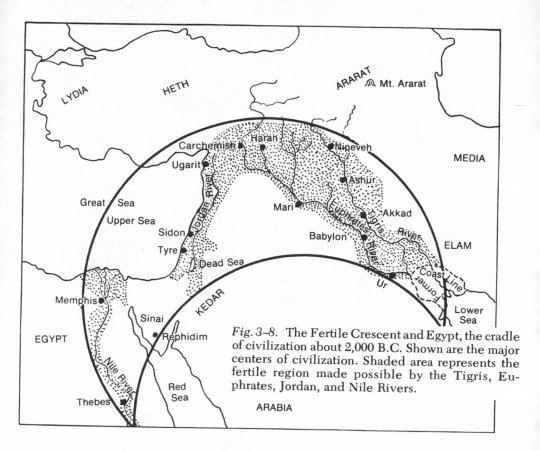

Fig. 3–8. The Fertile Crescent and Egypt, the cradle of civilization about 2,000 B.C. Shown are the major centers of civilization. Shaded area represents the fertile region made possible by the Tigris, Euphrates, Jordan, and Nile Rivers.

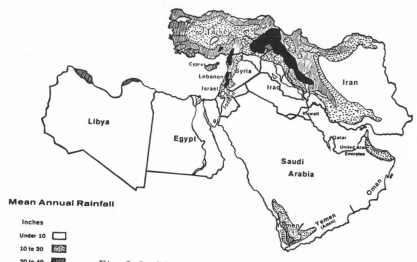

Mean Annual Rainfall

Inches

Under 10

10 to 20

20 to 40

Over 40

Fig. 3–9. Mean annual rainfall in a portion of the biblical lands today. Scientists say that, although there has been some fluctuation in rainfall occurrences, rainfall patterns are about the same as they were at the time of Abraham. CIA

the Hebrew conquest than they are today. Additionally, the semiarid areas bore woody vegetation where the soil and moisture conditions would permit (*Fig. 3–10*).

Flavius Josephus, the noted Jewish historian (A.D. 37?-c. 100) in speaking of the "Promised Land," said the area was like "a garden of God in which there grows the most precious and most beautiful trees in amazing varieties."

As to the area of Galilee (*Fig. 3–11*) where Christ had his home and where his ministry was mostly conducted, Josephus said: "The whole area is excellent for crops or cattle and rich in forests of every kind, so that by its adaptability it invites even those least inclined to work on the land" (*Fig. 3–12*).

The barren, treeless, arid landscapes of Judaea and Samaria (*Fig. 3–13*) so characteristic of the land today are unlike that of Josephus' time. He reports that the lands "are made up of hills and plains, with the soil easily worked and repaying cultivation. They are well wooded and prolific in fruit, both wild and cultivated; for nowhere is the soil arid by nature and rain is generally ample. All their streams are remarkably sweet, and lush grass is so plentiful that the milk-yield of their cows is exceptionally heavy. The final proof of their outstanding productivity is the swarming populations of Judaea and Samaria."

At the time of Moses the land east of the Jordan River, extending from the lower end of the Sea of Galilee to the northern end of the Dead Sea, and from the Jordan eastward to the desert, was a land of forests, grazing lands, and moisture. This region, known as Gilead, is a plateau about 2000 feet in elevation. It was from this area that Moses, standing on Mount Pisgah, was permitted to see the land of "milk and honey" by the Lord before his demise (Deut. 34:1). Gilead was noted for its forest products. It was an exporter of balm (Ezek. 27:17).

In referring to the mountains of Palestine, the noted biblical archeologist, Albright, said that in the Middle Bronze Age (2000–1500 B.C.), they were heavily forested on the

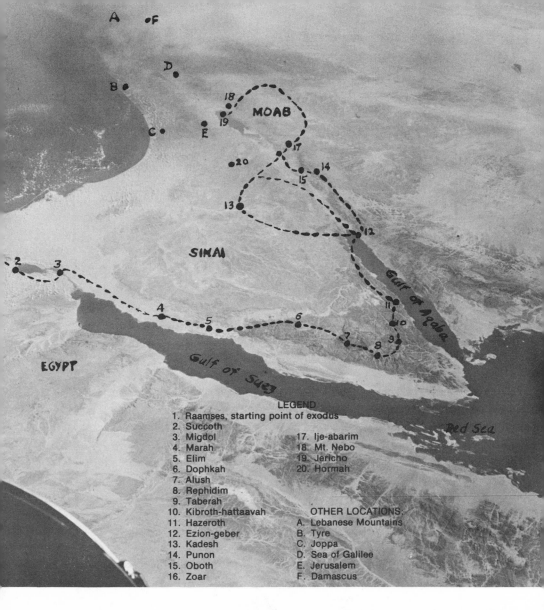

LEGEND
1. Raamses, starting point of exodus
2. Succoth
3. Migdol
4. Marah
5. Elim
6. Dophkah
7. Alush
8. Rephidim
9. Taberah
10. Kibroth-hattaavah
11. Hazeroth
12. Ezion-geber
13. Kadesh
14. Punon
15. Oboth
16. Zoar
17. Ije-abarim
18. Mt. Nebo
19. Jericho
20. Hormah

OTHER LOCATIONS:
A. Lebanese Mountains
B. Tyre
C. Joppa
D. Sea of Galilee
E. Jerusalem
F. Damascus

Fig. 3–10. Aerial view of the Sinai and the "land of milk and honey" as taken in 1966 by an astronaut on board Gemini XI. This area is generally considered as the Holy Land in contrast to the broad Mediterranean region which can be called the Bible lands. Dash line indicates the approximate route traveled by Moses during the Exodus; the exact route taken by the Israelites after they left Ezion-geber and before going around Moab to the Promised Land is not known because of their 40-year stay and wandering in this area. Moses referred to many trees and woody plants during his travels in the Sinai. NASA

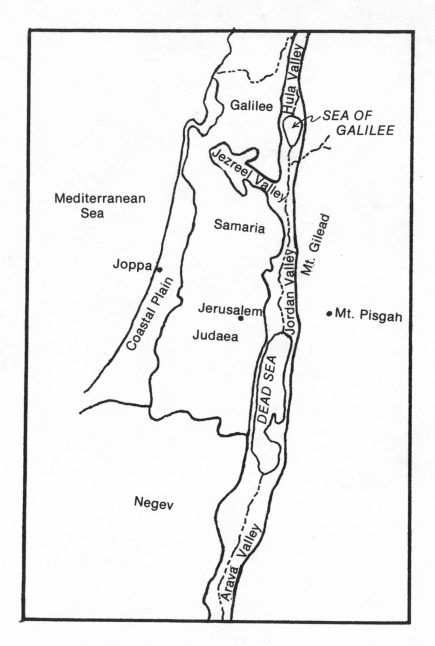

Fig. 3–11. Generalized geographic map of Israel.

Fig. 3–12. The Sea of Galilee showing once forested hills in background. Few visitors to this sea today realize that, at the time of Christ, the sea was much larger. Deforestation and intensive grazing caused serious erosion from the hills to fill in the former seashore. At the Kibbutz Tel Yosef the erosional fill is about eight feet in depth. CGI

Fig. 3–13. View of the Samarian hills northeast of Jerusalem today. They are still in partial agriculture. Extent of erosion is evident from rocks. Josephus, the historian, reports that this area was once well wooded, prolific in fruit and lush grass. CMC

watershed ridge and on the western slope so that there was little arable land.

Islands mentioned in the Bible were originally mountainous and wooded. Crete was called by Pliny the Elder A.D. 23–79) "the very home of cypress." The island of Cyprus provided many of the wood needs of the people in the early Bible days and still produces forest products.

More than 300 references are made to trees, groves, and forests in the Bible. Yet today, these are nonexistent for the most part. The famous cedars of Lebanon (*Fig. 3–14* and *3–15*) once covered an estimated 2000 square miles of land and are today limited to a few isolated small stands of trees within its original range. Generally, only trees associated with holy places were permitted to live and grow.

As related in the Bible, Abraham selected for his first exploration of Palestine the trail over the hills to the south. He did so since the forests offered a place of refuge and concealment from the Canaanites who lived in the plain below. Also, there was pasture for his flocks and herds in the hills.

David went to the forest of Hareth to conceal himself from Saul who sought to kill him (1 Sam. 22:5). Even Saul encamped in a forest near Beth-aven during his battle with the Philistines (1 Sam. 14:25).

Forest areas provided honey and served as a habitat for wild game animals (Ps. 50:10; Jer. 5:6; 1 Sam. 14:25, 26). Thus, these areas provided food to the forest dwellers. The psalmist refers to the power of God over the forests (Ps. 29:9).

Extensive forest areas in Ephraim, Lebanon, Carmel, Bashan, and Arabia, to name but a few, are referred to in the Scriptures (2 Sam. 18:6–8; 1 Kings 7:2; 2 Kings 19:23; Isa. 2:13; 21:13). The forests of Ephraim were large enough to conceal 20,000 men fleeing from battle, yet today they are nonexistent. The forest of Bashan was primarily made up of oak.

Joshua implies that the Hebrews found the central highlands heavily forested (Josh. 17:15, 18). Evidence that such was probably the case lies in the burning of Hazor. As reported in Joshua 11:11, 12, Joshua "burned Hazor with fire" as Moses, the servant of the Lord, had commanded. Hazor stood on a mound. A city of about 40,000 people, it had defense ramparts said to be close to 100 feet above a dry moat. Yet, though it appeared impregnable, Joshua conquered and burned it.

When the site was excavated by archeologists, about four feet of black ash earth and other material mixed with the soil was found. Said the noted James Kelso, a well-known archeologist: "We have never seen indications of a more destructive conflagration in any other Palestinian excavation, a fact which suggests extensive use of wood in construction at Bethel." Such extensive use of wood also indicates its availability in quantity from a local source.

Fig. 3–14. Cedars of Lebanon. Few residual stands remain today. This tree species once graced the mountains of Lebanon and its wood was an article of commerce throughout the known world during the biblical period. GG

Fig. 3–15. Present day topographic map showing the mountains of Lebanon which once supported dense stands of the famous cedars of Lebanon. CIA

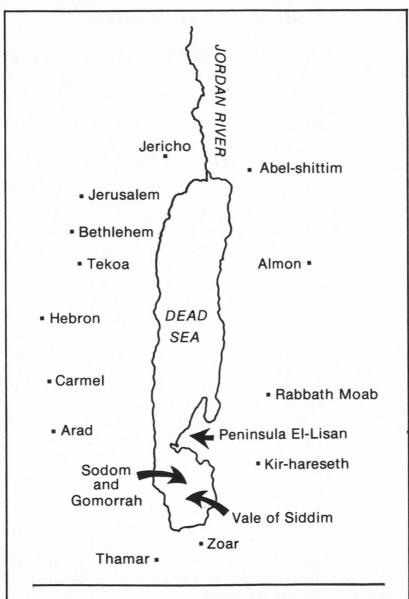

Fig. 3–16. Generalized map of the Dead Sea area. Sodom and Gomorrah are believed by biblical authorities to have been located in what is now the southern portion of the Dead Sea.

About 520 B.C. Haggai refers to the mountains having
sufficient wood for the construction of a new temple (Hag.
1:8). Jotham built castles and forts in the forests of Judah
(2 Chron. 27:4).

Based on the many biblical passages, there is sufficient
evidence to support the belief that in ancient times the
forests were more abundant than today.

Forest of the Dead Sea

Following the dispute between the herdsmen of Abram
and Lot near Beth-el over grazing lands, Abram suggested
they part ways, with the choice given to Lot (Gen. 13:6–9).
Lot chose the plain of Jordan while Abram, or Abraham as
he was later called, went east to the land of Canaan.

As Lot saw the land, he chose the portion that "—was
well watered every where . . . even as the garden of the
Lord, like the land of Egypt, as thou comest into Zoar"
(Gen. 13:10). Lot resided near Sodom in this plain.
Josephus refers to the area of Sodom as "of old a most
happy land, both for the fruits it bore and the riches of its
cities, although it be now burnt up."

While Lot gives a vivid description of a wonderful land
of "milk and honey," no word was said as to the forests of
the plain. Yet, they were there. Perhaps this was implied
by Lot's use of the word "garden" which is usually associated with trees.

Sodom and Gomorrah were inhabited by wicked people
and "the Lord rained upon Sodom and Gomorrah
brimstone and fire from the Lord out of heaven; and he
overthrew those cities and all the plain, and all the inhabitants of the cities, and that which grew upon the ground"
(Gen. 19:24, 25; cp. Jer. 50:40). Lot and his family escaped
this holocaust. Lot's wife, who disobeyed the Lord by looking back, was turned into a pillar of salt.

For centuries the location of Sodom and Gomorrah was
unknown to biblical scholars. Today they are considered to

lie under a part of the Dead Sea, the shallow portion from
the peninsula el Lisan to the southern tip (*Fig. 3–16*). It is
known as the Vale of Siddim, the land where the three
kings banded together (Gen. 14:3).

In this portion of the Dead Sea, when the sun is in the
right direction, a forest of salt-encrusted trees may be seen
beneath the waters. This attests to forests in this area of
Bible lands. The high salt content of the sea has preserved
them from the time that the cities of the plain were destroyed about 1900 B.C. This is about the time of Abraham.

Perhaps Lot was familiar with this forest area and at one
time may have grazed his large flocks under the branches
of the trees.

Tree Areas of Bible Lands before Interference by Man

What was the pattern of tree growth in biblical lands
before interference by man? While no one can say with
certainty, ecologists, considering climatic, edaphic, and
biotic factors, coupled with historical plant records, can
give a fairly reliable picture for the arid portion of early
Bible history. A comparison of present-day vegetation in
contrast to such vegetation before interference by man is
shown in *Fig. 3–17.*

For purposes of comparison the area shown on each map
is slightly larger than the land mass of the original 48 states
of the United States.

It becomes obvious from a review of the maps that, while
tree and grass areas never did occupy much of the total
land area, there has been a radical reduction in the major
vegetative cover, and especially of forests and other tree
areas. Barren desert areas have increased in size.

Egypt, the land of the Nile, never did have many forest
resources and had to rely on other nations for her vital
wood needs throughout history. On the other hand, the
Jordan River region was blessed with plentiful wood resources.

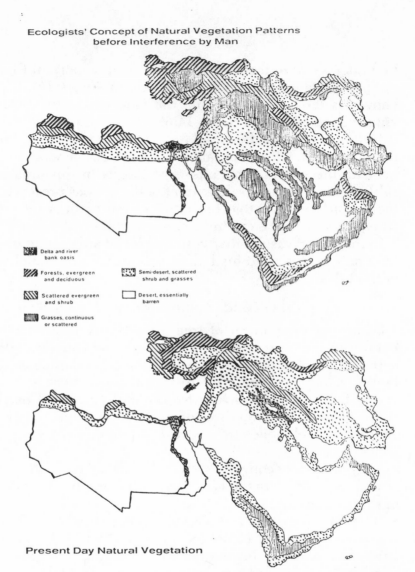

Ecologists' Concept of Natural Vegetation Patterns
before Interference by Man

Delta and river
bank oasis

Forests, evergreen
and deciduous

Scattered evergreen
and shrub

Grasses, continuous
or scattered

Semi-desert, scattered
shrub and grasses

Desert, essentially
barren

Present Day Natural Vegetation

Fig. 3–17. A comparison of natural vegetation present today throughout the Bible lands in contrast to its condition before interference by man. CIA

Probably the trees from the forests, in what today is called Libya *(Fig. 3–18),* were also an article of commerce

Fig. 3–18. Atlas cedar, *Cedrus atlantica,* growing in the Mediterranean mountain area of northeast Algeria. This species also grew originally in the Mediterranean coastal mountains of what is today called Tunisia and Libya. It is related to the cedar of Lebanon. Though limited in commercial area, the wood from the Atlas cedar was no doubt an item of commerce with ancient Egypt. USFS, USDA

with Egypt. The French explorer August Chevalier found traces of dense forests that existed less than 2000 years ago beneath the sands of the Sahara.

What is today known as Timgad, in Algeria, was once a flourishing city of the Romans. It was called Thamugadi. Formerly, forests were common to the area. It supported extensive olive orchards. As they did with other parts of North Africa, the Romans turned the area into a grain basket to feed the Roman population. Forests and olive orchards were destroyed to provide an increasing amount of grain on submarginal land. The land was overworked, the hills overgrazed. Soon the wind took over, blowing the soil which was left. The result was that Thamugadi was buried under the sand until it was excavated some 1300 years later (Fig. 3–19).

Other biblical lands such as Italia, Silicia, Macedonia, Achaia, and Crete, not shown on the map, were extensively forested during the biblical period.

There can be no doubt that man, through his misuse of the natural resources, including trees, as well as God's judgments, have adversely affected man's habitat and his way of life.

Effect of Climate on Vegetative Changes

There is a prevailing view that climatic changes have reduced once-productive areas of grass and tree vegetation to the condition which exists today. This is not the view of scientists, however. While there has been some fluctuation in rainfall occurrences, the climate in the Middle East has, for many centuries, remained stable. Actually, knowledgeable scientists say that regional climates, in a broad sense, have improved and that the amount of rainfall has increased since antiquity, and yet deserts continue to spread and large areas become more arid as time goes on. Man

Fig. 3–19. The Roman city of Thamugadi in north Africa, prior to its exploitation by the Romans, was a land supporting coastal forests, extensive olive orchards and grazing. The Romans used the land to produce vast quantities of grain, and the land was overworked. The soil began to shift with the winds. What was once a productive area was buried and no longer of value to man (sketch courtesy Gene Coulter and the Wyoming Game and Fish Commission).

himself brought on and continues to bring on changes in his environment.

It is reasonable to assume that climatic factors, especially rainfall, have played a major role in present-day vegetative patterns in the holy lands. Most of the lands are arid and receive less than ten inches of rainfall annually.

In general, the Mediterranean climate features a small amount of rainfall, warm summer temperatures, and long dry seasons.

4 ✻✻✻✻✻✻✻✻✻✻✻✻✻✻✻

✻ Factors Contributing to the Decrease of Tree Resources and Environmental Changes in Bible Lands

IN GRIEF AND MISERY, and despised by all, Job blamed God for man's mistakes. He has not been the last person to do so. Said Job: "The waters wear the stones: thou washeth away the things which grow out of the dust of the earth; and thou destroyeth the hope of man" (Job 14:19).

Irresponsibility of Man

It is evident from the pages of history, including the Bible, that, contrary to Job's statement, natural resource mismanagement by man himself resulted in the de-terioration of civilizations *(Fig. 4–1)* or the decay and dis-appearance of civilizations through carelessness, usually by unthinking acts and often as a result of greed. Long-abandoned ruins of mighty civilizations under the sands of time, barren slopes, ever-spreading deltas and man-made deserts are testimonies to man's misuse of his natural re-

Fig. 4–1. Ancient Greece became a powerful and influential nation. It was a land of beautiful cities. The arts flourished. The bases of its greatness were its forests and an ample water supply, coupled with rich, productive soils. The Greeks failed to see their dependency on these resources, and abused and overworked them. Actually, tillers' work was held in disdain. When the forests were removed, once regulated clear streams no longer existed. Today, Greece does not have a natural resource base that once made her great. She is a vivid reminder of man's mismanagement of natural resources (sketch courtesy Gene Coulter and Wyoming Game and Fish Commission).

sources, including forests, trees, shrubs, and other green plants. Such resource mismanagement in arid and semiarid areas continues today and has resulted in action by the United Nations to stem the tide of desert encroachment.

Population Concentration

Man did not set out consciously to destroy his environment. At first he hunted animals and used these along with berries and other fruits and roots as food. He traveled from one point to another and had little impact on his environment. Neither did his primitive agriculture have any effect, since the land was not taxed to the limit. It was only when man settled and concentrated in large numbers in the valleys of the rivers and streams that abuse of the natural resources occurred. Agricultural land along rivers and streams was used more intensively year after year. Trees and shrubs on the mountains and hills were cut down to provide not only man's wood needs, but to allow for the expansion of agriculture on the slopes. Sheep and goats in increasing numbers were allowed to graze the hilly areas. The results, as described by Job, were inevitable. Man did not practice wise use. And, as man developed more sophistication and skills, the greater grew his power over nature and the more potentially destructive he became.

Archeologists have stated that, in arid and semiarid areas, the use of local timber for building of entire villages radically changed the composition of the tree vegetation, particularly in areas where the trees have a slow growth rate. This is evident in the arid regions of Israel where some species disappeared and others greatly reduced in numbers following exploitation by man to provide for an expanding population.

Failure to Understand the Role of Trees and Other Plants

The people of the biblical period either failed to understand or cared little about the role which trees and woody shrubs on the mountains and hills played in sustaining their present or future way of life. These plants held the soil together through their extensive root systems. The tree leaves which fell to the ground kept the soil from drying out, and in the process of decaying, replaced minerals in the soil to enrich it to support later plant growth. The plant environment also permitted the soil to soak up water and serve as a regulator of stream flow. Additionally, the forested areas provided food and a habitat for birds and game animals.

Of regional importance is the fact that the lack of moisture in the ground means less will be evaporated back into clouds. This can lead to less rainfall. As a result, once-fertile regions can turn gradually into wastelands.

Scientists with the National Center for Atmospheric Research say that satellite photographs have provided proof of the effects of overgrazing and large scale operations to clear land of timber and other vegetation. The ground in such deforested areas loses much of its capacity to hold and store water.

The famous cedars of Lebanon, for example, once densely covered the mountains of ancient Phoenicia (*Fig. 4-2*). They were indiscriminately and destructively cut for domestic use and as a product of commerce throughout the then known world. Perhaps the trees were deemed inexhaustible, as was the feeling of people during the colonial period of American history. Or, perhaps they "mined" the resource without regard to its future, to get the maximum short-term value. At any rate, no thought was given to the regeneration of the cedar and other species associated with the cedar which had much economic and social value. Apparently, past lessons of history went unheeded.

With the deforestation of the land, erosion commenced. Overgrazing by sheep and goats prevented the tree seedlings from forming new forests and further aggravated the erosion process. By cropping the grass close to the ground, and by compacting the soil and tearing it up, the animals caused the soil to become subject to movement by the slightest forces of wind or rain. The soil and water relationship was altered, with the soil holding less water. Soils bare of vegetation were exposed to the sunlight. As a result, water evaporated faster, land became drier, soil temperatures rose, organisms within the soil were altered, water tables were lowered, and wells and springs were affected. Birds and wildlife common to the region disappeared. All the interrelationships of life and the environment were changed. The land was less productive and less capable of providing the needs of the people.

Fig. 4–2. The cedars of Lebanon were destructively cut for commercial use throughout the known world by the Phoenicians. Shown is the characteristic branching of the young trees (photo courtesy Hal Harris).

Fig. 4–3. The number of sheep and goats in Bible lands was prodigious during the biblical period. Overgrazing by these animals prevented tree seedlings from forming new forests and aggravated the erosion process. The results are evident today. Unfortunately, such uncontrolled grazing still exists on many areas of these lands. SL

The extensiveness of grazing during the Bible period is reflected in many biblical passages. The number of animals was prodigious (Fig. 4–3). Solomon offered 120,000 sheep during the dedication and consecration of the Temple (1 Kings 8:63). The king of Moab paid a tribute of 200,000 lambs and rams (2 Kings 3:4). Reuben took 250,000 sheep from the children of Ishmael (1 Chron. 5:21).

While the process of resource loss occurred in the Phoenician mountains, it had equal application on hills and mountains throughout the Bible region where there were trees and other plants (Fig. 4–4).

Today, many hills formerly densely forested with "cedars of Lebanon" are barren and devoid of soil. The absence of soil in a residual stand of cedar will be noted in Figure 3–14.

Forest and grass fires purposely set by the nomads in an act of destruction, or through acts of carelessness or maliciousness by others, also contributed to the loss of trees.

Syria, famous in biblical times for its oaks, contains the ruins of Jerash buried under deep erosional soils, the result of mismanagement of the land resources. At one time, according to archeologists, Jerash was reported to be a city of about 250,000 people. The ruins of over 100 other large cities in ancient Syria attest to its prosperity at an early period in history (Fig. 4–5). It was a nation that exported timber and large quantities of wine and olive oil.

Cain-and-Abel Struggle

From the beginning of time there has been a "Cain-and-Abel" struggle between the shepherd and farmer, the tent-dweller and home-dweller. These conflicts account, in part, for the tragic destruction of trees and plants in many areas. Raids and invasions by nomads from the grasslands and the desert upon the farming people and city-dwellers of the plains brought devastation and destruction not only to the cities, but to any conservation practices initiated by the plains people.

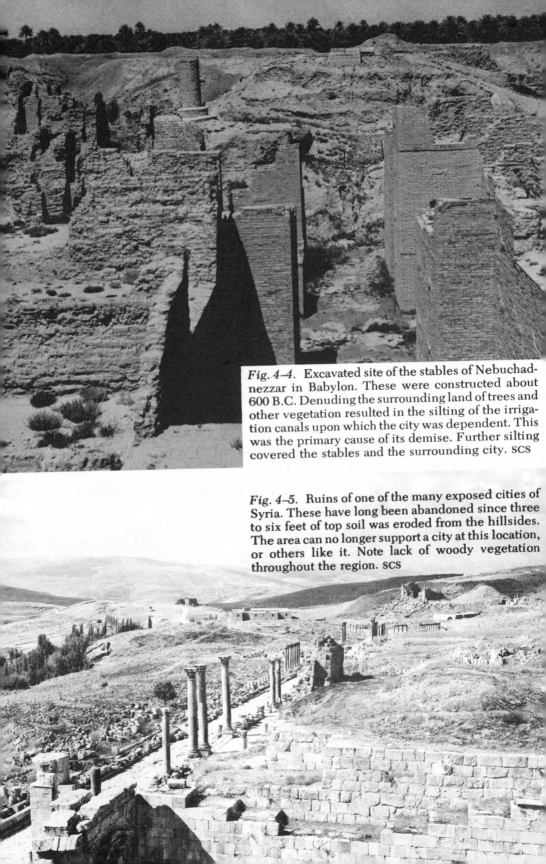

Fig. 4-4. Excavated site of the stables of Nebuchadnezzar in Babylon. These were constructed about 600 B.C. Denuding the surrounding land of trees and other vegetation resulted in the silting of the irrigation canals upon which the city was dependent. This was the primary cause of its demise. Further silting covered the stables and the surrounding city. SCS

Fig. 4-5. Ruins of one of the many exposed cities of Syria. These have long been abandoned since three to six feet of top soil was eroded from the hillsides. The area can no longer support a city at this location, or others like it. Note lack of woody vegetation throughout the region. SCS

When the nomads invaded a city they dispersed the inhabitants, filled up the wells, destroyed all the trees, and burned up the vegetation. What was once a fruitful spot became, under the burning sun, an area covered with saline efflorescense, the forerunner of future sterility (*Fig. 4–6*).

The fact that tree and woody shrub areas border on deserts always made forested areas subject to heavy damage by the nomads. Excessive browsing by their goats damaged bud-bearing branches and deformed the trees, making them shrublike. This is no doubt a factor which, under Mediterranean conditions, has converted forests with large trees to shrubs.

Feuds Between Kings

Likewise, feuds between tribal chiefs also contributed to resource loss through the burning and destruction of trees as well as other property (Judg. 9:45). In biblical days feuds between towns and cities were unending. There was no supreme authority. Each chief was master of his own territory. The Bible refers to them as kings. Insofar as power and independence were concerned, that is what they were. Relationships between tribal chiefs and subjects were patriarchal. Within the walls of the city lived the king, the aristocracy, the king's representatives, and wealthy merchants.

Devastation wrought upon the land and its resources is indicated by the three Israelite kings who overran Moab. Demolishing the cities, they destroyed the fields, and filled them with rocks from the brooks. They stopped up the wells and felled all the best trees. Finally they overthrew the walls of the city to their foundations (2 Kings 3:25).

Tiglath-pileser, King of Assyria, who defeated the wicked King Ahaz of Judah in battle, bragged about his destruction of trees. Archeologists found a record which said: "The tribute of Ahaz the Judean I received, gold,

Fig. 4–6. In many parts of the Bible lands where deserts prevail, the ecological balance of nature is very fragile. In situations where nomads invaded and destroyed a community by cutting down its trees, destroying the surrounding area by fire, filling up its wells, and killing its people, what was once a fruitful spot became an area of sterility and desolation. Evidence of unstable soil as a result of ecological changes is pictured. CGI

silver, lead, tin and linen. Damascus I destroyed. Rezin I took. His officers I empaled alive on stakes. I hewed down his orchards, nor did I leave a tree standing." This statement parallels the event recorded in 2 Kings 16 and Isaiah 7.

No doubt kings also resorted to arson fires of grazing lands and forests when it suited their purpose for conquest. Other examples of feuds which destroyed the natural resource base will be noted throughout the book.

Use of Wood for Fuel and Kilns

It has been said that the liberal use of wood for fuel and for brick kilns over the centuries contributed greatly to the barrenness of land. Of this there can be little doubt.

Universally, man has used wood for fuel or to make charcoal with which to cook his meals and heat his shelters. Wood was scarce in many parts of Bible lands and consequently any combustible material was welcome for his use (Ps. 58:9; Eccl. 7:6; Isa. 9:5; Ezek. 4:12–15). Generally, wood was particularly desired because it would burn longer. Thus, it was much sought after.

Even today more than one-half of the world's wood harvest is used to build warming or cooking fires. According to the United Nations, nine-tenths of the people in most poor countries depend on firewood as their chief source of fuel. They also report that for more than one-third of the world's population, their crisis is a daily scramble to find the wood they need to cook their meals.

While a brick kiln is mentioned by Jeremiah (43:9), Egyptian bricks were generally dried in the sun as were those in Nineveh. Babylonian bricks, however, were more commonly baked in a kiln and were the principal material used in construction of buildings. Each brick was stamped on the flat side by the use of incised wooden blocks with the name of the sovereign.

Bricks were generally used in the Euphrates and Tigris

river areas and other regions devoid of other building material such as stone.

Perhaps one of the most important facilities using bricks prepared in brick kilns was the city of Babylon. Built by Nebuchadnezzar who ruled from 606–561 B.C., it was one of the wonders of the world. Its greatness is attested by the Book of Daniel. Herodotus informs us that the walls around the city were 60 miles in length. It was a square, with each side being 15 miles long. The walls were 75 feet in width and 300 feet in height. Surrounding the walls of the city was a vast ditch, lined with brick. Within the walls were great edifices, the royal palace with its famous hanging garden and the temple of Belus, also constructed of brick. Considering other constructions within the city, it is obvious that an immense amount of wood would be needed to provide the heat for the millions of bricks manufactured in the king's kilns. Obviously, the forest resources available to the king were badly depleted as a result.

The first mention of bricks in the Bible is the account of the building of the tower of Babel (Gen. 11:3).

Use of Wood in Warfare

The use of wood as an article of warfare is shown by Nebuchadnezzar's punitive campaign against the rebellious Judah, and especially against the walled city of Lachish (2 Kings 25:1; Jer. 34:7).

James Lesley Starkey, the archeologist who excavated Lachish in 1938, found wood ashes in layers several yards thick which, after 2500 years, were higher than the remains of the solid limestone walls of the fallen city.

Apparently Nebuchadnezzar's engineers were specialists in the art of fire. For miles around Lachish the forests were cleared of all woody vegetation and brought to the walls of the city. The material was stacked to the height of a house all around the walls and set on fire. Additional material was added as needed. The fire raged day and night and ringed the walls from top to bottom. Much wood was used for this purpose. The fire was kept up until the hot limestone walls burst and caved in.

It is obvious that all the trees around Lachish, including olive trees, were cut down and used in the fire since Starkey found many charred olive stones among the ashes.

What an area of utter destruction this region must have been after the fall of Lachish!

The same technique could not be used against the walled city of Jerusalem by the Babylonians since the forest resources around the city had been earlier reduced through overcutting, grazing, and agriculture.

When, in the year A.D. 70, the Romans laid seige to Jerusalem (Luke 21:5, 6, 20, 23, 24), Titus made a last bid for surrender by sending their captive countryman, Josephus, to ask them to lay down their arms. The Jews refused. Titus therefore gave orders to crucify all who were caught outside the wall, either deserters, raiders, or foragers. Over 500 a day were nailed to crosses just outside the city until a lack of wood called a halt to this practice.

As with the city of Lachish, the Romans scoured the region around Jerusalem for miles to secure the wood needed for crosses, siege ramps, scaling ladders, and camp fires. Fig and olive trees were not spared, nor did the Mount of Olives provide the shade it once did after this conquest.

As Josephus said, "No stranger who had seen Judaea of old, and the lovely suburbs of its capitol, and now saw this devastation could have restrained his tears and lamentations at the hideous change."

Josephus, an army commander of the Hebrews, made these interesting remarks with respect to the use of wood in warfare: "When you have pitched your camp, take care that you do nothing that is cruel. And when you are engaged in a siege, and want timber for the making of warlike engines, do not you render the land naked by cutting down trees that bear fruit, but spare them, as considering that they were made for the benefit of men; and that if they could speak, they would have a just plea against you, because, though they are not occasions of the war, they are unjustly treated, and suffer in it, and would, if they were able, remove themselves into another land."

The practice of cutting down or taking trees out of the ground by the roots was forbidden, even in small wars, by the law of Moses (Deut. 20:19, 20). Yet, it was allowed by God in the case of the Moabites as a punishment for their wickedness.

Josephus, when a commander, and in defense of Jotapata from the Romans under Vespasian, cut down all trees on the mountain that adjoined the city.

In Ezekiel's prophecies (Ezek. 39:9, 10) it is evident that wood will play a significant role in the final battle when the enemy Gog is destroyed by God. The weapons and vehicles of the soldiers are described by him as being made primarily from wood.

Ezekiel also states that the weapons and vehicles will serve as firewood for a period of seven years after the close of the battle. Said Ezekiel: "And they that dwell in the cities of Israel shall go forth, and shall set on fire and burn the weapons, both the shields and the bucklers, and bows and the arrows, and the handstaves, and the spears, and they shall burn them with fire seven years: so that they shall take no wood out of the field, neither cut down any of the forests; for they shall burn the weapons with fire: and they shall spoil those that spoiled them, and rob those that robbed them, saith the Lord God."

5

🍁 Importance of Tree Resources in Biblical Lands

THE TREES AND WOODY PLANTS of the Bible lands served man in many ways. In addition to his three basic needs they provided many hundreds of simple luxuries and necessities *(Fig. 5–1)*. Some of the uses of wood mentioned in the Bible include: wagons (1 Sam. 6:14), chariots (1 Sam. 13:5; 2 Kings 6:14), threshing sledges (1 Chron. 21:23), wooden utensils (Lev. 16:12), yokes (Jer. 27:2; 28:13), furniture (Exod. 25:9–28), household vessels (Exod. 7:19; Lev. 15:12; 2 Tim. 2:20), musical instruments (1 Kings 10:12), wood for carving (Exod. 31:5; 35:33), and employment (1 Kings 5:1–18; Deut. 19:5).

In Egypt, boomerangs and carved sticks made of wood were used for hunting. Surprisingly, well-to-do families provided their children with many wooden toys such as dolls with movable parts, rattles, and whistles. Some of the dolls had lifelike hair.

Fig. 5–1. An oasis was an area sought by a traveler in the desert. It was here that he could find water, rest in the shade, and find food in season. One of the most important tree resources in the Bible, the date palm, grows in an oasis. Pictured is an oasis in the Negev desert. CGI

Wood was extensively used as fuel and there are many biblical references to this. For milleniums trees were the only source of fuel for cooking, heating, and lime kilns.

From trees man secured the medicine, oils, dyes, and other products used in his daily life. A discussion of these will follow in a subsequent chapter. Implements of war were also made from trees (Num. 36:18; 2 Chron. 26:15). Unfortunately, trees and other plants also provided poisons misused by man for his personal gain. While the Bible is silent on this matter, other historians point out their use to kill others. Perhaps the best known case is that of Socrates who drank hemlock poison while in prison.

Greek and Roman farmers are known to have used chemicals available from plants and trees in their battle against insect pests. No doubt those of more ancient times used similar methods.

Primitive man, using crude instruments, made dugout boats from tree trunks. This permitted him to extend his range of exploration. Gradually these boats became larger and more efficient, permitting him to travel to far distant points in search of trade goods and to war upon others. Up until the middle of the last century boats were made entirely of wood. It can be said that wood helped to influence the course of history.

Wood was extensively used for religious purposes by the heathen and by the Hebrews.

A fire of "fir" wood was kept constantly burning on an altar before the golden statue of Apollo.

During the Jewish feast of Xylophory, in the reign of Agrippa, it was the custom for everyone to bring wood for the altar "that there might never be a want of fuel for the fire which was unquenchable and always burning," according to Josephus.

In the time of Moses, it was the function of the priests to keep a perpetual fire burning upon the altar. Speaking to Moses, the Lord said: "And the fire upon the altar shall be burning in it; it shall not be put out: and the priest shall burn wood on it every morning, and lay the burnt offering

Fig. 5–2. A cedar of Lebanon tree located in a cemetery in northeast Texas. Because of its beauty and biblical background, this species has been planted as an ornamental throughout the world where adaptable to the site. TFS

in order upon it; and he shall burn thereon the fat of the peace offerings" (Lev. 6:12).

In the forests were game and these provided a source of food. Hunting the game also provided a sport for kings and the elite.

Forests were of economic importance to the nations which controlled them. Through the export of timber products they were able to acquire other necessities in exchange.

During ancient periods there were appointed by rulers, "keepers of the royal forests." These individuals may be called the first "foresters." Herodotus, the famous Greek historian (484–424 B.C.) who accompanied Nehemiah to Judah, reports that King Artaxerxes gave Nehemiah a letter to be given to Asaph on their arrival in Jerusalem. Asaph was the keeper of the royal Lebanese forests. The letter authorized Nehemiah to secure such timber as he might need for rebuilding the walls and gates of Jerusalem (Neh. 2:4–8).

The trees of the Bible land also provided many social values which may not have been fully appreciated by all the people. They helped to regulate the temperature and climate in the area where they grew. The trees also aided in the conservation of water supply and in flood control through the prevention of run-off. Deep roots held the soil in check and prevented erosion.

Isaiah recognized the importance of trees in beautification (*Fig. 5–2*) in his exhortation: "The glory of Lebanon shall come unto thee, the fir tree, the pine tree, and the box together, to beautify the place of my sanctuary" (Isa. 60:13).

Forests served as a shelter from drying winds and provided food and habitat for wildlife. Trees also had recreational value for man.

Man was, and is continuing to be, dependent upon trees in his daily life.

Evidence of the scarcity and value of forests in Bible

lands is indicated by a historical note that goes back to 480 B.C. when Xerxes, the king of Persia, conquered Greece. The poor people from the plains of Attica immediately migrated to the city of Athens for the protection they thought the city would provide. Of particular interest is that they brought with them the wooden doors of their homes, one of their most prized possessions. Stone was readily available to construct their homes, but wood was a scarce commodity for the construction of doors. Apparently the forests then existing were insufficient to supply the wood needed for this simple luxury.

In 701 B.C. Sennacherib, the Assyrian king, invaded Judah (2 Kings 18:13–19, 36). In fear, Hezekiah gave tribute of immense wealth to Sennacherib. Included in this tribute were wood and wood products. So says the report of Sennacherib's scribes as found by archeologists. From the Bible we learn that the tribute was given at Lachish (1 Kings 18:14). Thus we see the importance attached to tree resources.

6

◊ Biblical References
to Trees
and
Woody Plants of the Bible

THROUGHOUT THE BIBLE many references are made to trees and woody plants identifiable today. There are others, however, on which authorities can only speculate as to the genus or species intended. One example of the latter is the gopher wood used by Noah in the construction of the ark. There is some general agreement among biblical scholars that it was cypress, a wood then commonly used in shipbuilding. Recent speculation, based on a piece of wood found in 1969 on Mount Ararat, is that it may have been oak. However, this has not found acceptance among authorities. Scientists have determined that the wood is but 1200 years old.

Many trees and woody plants common to Bible lands were not mentioned in the Scriptures. One authority has said there are over 850 genera and 3500 species of plants, with many plants yet to be classified. Numbered among these are many trees and woody plants. It is understandable that the authors of the Bible were not concerned with making the Bible a plant catalog.

Writers of the Bible used common terms as we do today, and a name in one area of the land would not necessarily be the same in another. Even in our own country there is confusion among lay persons as to accepted common names. Frequently, in parts of the South, the southern red oak, willow oak, and water oak are mistakenly referred to by some as "pin oaks." There are those who refer to several species of oaks as "Spanish oak." The junipers are miscalled "cedars." Even the lowly prickly ash is called tooth-ache tree, tickle-tongue, or prickly tree throughout its range. And who would recognize "farkleberry," the now accepted common name for tree huckleberry?

Fortunately today, through the use of scientific names given to plants with certain floral characteristics, we can identify an individual species irrespective of the common name used.

There follows a listing, brief descriptions, uses, and general information about trees and other woody plants referred to in the Bible. A few exceptions will be noted, and the reason for their inclusion will be obvious in a review of the text. Additionally, the names of products of some trees will be noted in the listing. This has been done to associate the product with the tree which was unnamed in the Bible. The listing is not intended to be a technical presentation although some scientific names are used.

The listing of plants is presented in this portion of the text so that the reader will be more familiar with the plants in the discussion which follows in subsequent chapters.

Acacia

The acacia tree of the Bible, otherwise known as desert acacia, shittam, shitta, shittim, or shittah, *Acacia raddiana*, ranges in height from about 8 to 18 feet. It is one of three

evergreen species of acacia said to be native to the Sinai
(*Fig. 6–1*). The other two are A. *seyal* and A. *tortilis*.

As with other members of the acacia family, of which the
black locust common to our country is included, the wood
is hard, orange colored, and insect resistant. When pol-
ished it makes a beautiful decorative wood.

Acacia species, hardy in nature, are characteristic of wilderness waste areas (*Fig. 6–2*). Catclaw and huisache are
but two species found in the semiarid areas of the south-
western United States.

The desert acacia yielded the wood that went into the
building of the Ark of the Covenant and into the first tabernacle (Exod. 36:20–23; 37:1)

It has been stated that desert acacia was probably used
for the ark since it was the only available wood. While this
may or may not have been the case, and the statement is
questionable in view of the presence of other known
species, no better wood could have been chosen to serve
the purpose in terms of durability. Josephus says the wood
chosen "would not decay by putrefaction" and was "naturally strong and could not be corrupted."

The desert acacia served other purposes. Its wood was
used to provide clamps for Egyptian mummy cases. From
it charcoal was made. The leaves and fruit of the tree
served as food for cattle, while its astringent bark was used
for the tanning of leather. Archeological studies show that
acacia, A. *raddiana*, was extensively used as a building
material.

Another acacia, native to Africa, *Acacia senegal*, is one
that produces the finest quality gum arabic. The exudation
from the tree is slowly soluble in water and has a high
degree of adhesiveness and viscosity. We are acquainted
with gum arabic in the adhesive of postage stamps.

The biblical name Beth-shitta means, literally, "house of
acacia." Other place names such as Shittim and Abel-
shittim are said to have been derived from the acacia which
once grew in abundance in these areas.

Fig. 6–1. Acacia tree growing near Timna in the Sinai, north of the Gulf of Eilat. It was from the acacia tree that Moses secured the wood for building the Ark of the Covenant.

Fig. 6–2. Present distribution pattern of acacia trees in a part of the Sinai desert. Presumably, acacia along with other tree species were used by Solomon to smelt copper for which he was famous. CMC

For centuries acacia, and other green plants, have been used in funeral services throughout the world as a symbol of immortality or resurrection. In some instances they may have been used as a tribute to the dead or for other spiritual effect.

Algum

There are several scriptural references to algum or almug trees. Yet there is no agreement among authorities as to the species of the tree intended. There is agreement, however, that "algum" and "almug" are one and the same tree.

It was from the land of Ophir that ships brought to Solomon a great supply of almug (1 Kings 10:11, 12; 2 Chron. 9:10, 11). From this wood Solomon made pillars for the Temple and the palace, harps, and harpsichords. There is no doubt that the wood was rare and unusual since it was mentioned that "never before, or since, was such almug trees seen."

It is of interest to note that, in two scriptural passages on the same event in the King James Version of the Bible, one refers to "almug" trees while the other says "algum" trees (1 Kings 10:11, 12; 2 Chron. 9:10, 11).

Josephus said that algum wood resembled the wood of a fir tree, but with a whiter and brighter sheen.

Weight of authority is that the algum was the red sandalwood of India, *Sabtalum album;* such is referred to in the Living Bible for the Chronicles passage. There is, however, only circumstantial evidence to substantiate this belief. As found in commerce today there is no doubt as to the suitability of sandalwood for making pillars, staircases, or harps.

Red sandalwood is used in China and India as an odoriferous substance to perfume temples and the houses of Sanskrit.

The land of Ophir is unknown, though presumed by some to be a part of Africa. If it could be reliably established, the identity of the species of algum could be more definitely determined.

One biblical reference tends to show that algum trees grew in Lebanon (2 Chron. 2:8). Solomon, when he was preparing to build the Temple, made a request for Hiram "to send me also cedar trees, fir trees, and algum trees out of Lebanon." This would seem to indicate that, during this period in history, algum was growing in the area, and was similar to that imported from Ophir. The tree may have been of poorer quality and now extinct. The algum could have been planted in a forest plantation by Hiram, King of Tyre, years before because of the tree's scarcity.

Almond

The almond, *Prunus amygdalus (Fig. 6–3),* is best known in the Bible in connection with the rod of Aaron (Num. 17:8). It was Aaron's almond rod which brought forth buds, produced blossoms, and yielded almonds in the matter of one day. This act attested the Lord's acceptance of Levi and the tribe of Levi to perform the religious duties.

Aaron's rod was preserved in the Holy of Holies and represented a tribute to God's provision for his children and was a symbol for a new national hope (Jer. 1:11, 12).

It was the flowers of the almond *(Fig. 6–4)* that contributed their graceful shape to the design of the sacred seven-branched candlestick of the Tabernacle (Exod. 25:32–38) *(Fig. 6–5).*

In other biblical passages the almond is used as a token of times out of date (Ezek. 7:10) and as a symbol of old age (Eccl. 12:5). The latter may refer to the white hair of age. The almond tree has the appearance of the head of an old man when the profuse white or pinkish flowers appear before the advent of the leaves.

Reportedly there are four species of wild almond indigenous to Bible lands. One authority says that the almond probably had its origin in India or Persia but the weight of authority is against this.

Fig. 6–3. Almond growing in an uncultivated area in Israel planted to aleppo pine. Note extension of erosion that has taken place on this site in the past. CGI

Fig. 6–5. The Menorah, a well-known Jewish symbol, is patterned after the seven-branched candlestick constructed by Moses in the Sinai desert upon the command of God. The instructions to Moses were presented in specific botanical terms that used almond as a basis of the pattern. The High Priest was commanded to fill the candlestick with pure olive oil and to burn it perpetually in the Tent of Meeting.

Fig. 6–4. The flowers of the almond contributed their graceful shape to the design of the sacred seven-branched candlestick of the Tabernacle as constructed by Moses (photo courtesy California Almond Growers Exchange).

At the St. Catherine Monastery in southern Sinai, well preserved wood dating from the sixth century shows that almond was extensively used in its construction. Other species similarly used were date palm, poplar, and cypress. The use of almond as a building material is surprising in that it is a highly valuable fruit tree. Its use in the Monastery indicates that, at the time of Christ, there was an overabundance of almond trees in the mountains.

Almond found growing naturally in the Sinai mountains could account for the adoption, by the Hebrews, of almond branches as a model of the lampstand (Exod. 25:33–36).

It is known that Jacob sent almonds, among other items, to Joseph in Egypt as a gift, in return for food and the release of his son Benjamin (Gen. 43:11).

In form and blossom the almond tree resembles a peach tree. Its Hebrew name is "waker," alluding to its being the first fruit tree to put forth blossoms after the winter season.

The tender, acidious, unripe crisp pod was eaten as a food in Bible lands. More important, however, were the ripe almonds with which we in this nation are familiar. From the nuts, almond oil was derived to flavor food, much as in our day. The oil was also used as an ointment. There are two major varieties of almond trees, one producing sweet, the other bitter almonds. Almond extract is prepared from the sweet almonds.

The almond thrives in Syria today and is in commercial production in many parts of the world, including the United States. It also thrives in Palestine and other countries of the Near East. Many varieties have been cultivated since ancient times.

Almond nuts and almond oil were important items of trade in ancient Greece and Rome. Archeological evidence, from ships which sank in the Mediterranean Sea as early as 2000 B.C., indicate that almonds were an item of commerce in this period.

Almug

This was the wood imported from Ophir by Hiram, King of Tyre, for use in Solomon's temple and for other purposes. Refer to discussion under "algum."

Aloes

Aloes, *Aquilaria agallocha,* otherwise known as lign aloes or lignum aloes, is a large tree common to Sylhet in East Bengal. Its wood contains a resin and essential oil that has been prized since antiquity. Similar substances are produced from other trees of the same genus in India and China and used accordingly *(Fig. 6–6).*

Aloes is mentioned four times in the Old Testament and once in the New Testament. In Numbers it is likened to the tents of Israel (Num. 24:6). An extract from the plant was used as a perfume for garments (Ps. 45:8) and was a

Fig. 6–6. Aloes trees growing in India, its native habitat. From such trees are derived a resin and an oil that has been prized by kings since antiquity. Such oil was part of the holy ointment used by the Hebrews. Nicodemus came to the tomb of Jesus bringing both the aloes and myrrh to prepare his body for burial. BPS

part of the holy ointment used by the Hebrews (Song of Sol. 4:14). Aloes was well known to the Greeks and Arabians and highly prized for its perfume.

While the tree was not originally native to the holy lands, it is obvious that it was grown in gardens in the Jordan Valley (Song of Sol. 4:12–14). Historical records indicate that many trees (which have long since disappeared) were once cultivated in this area.

Obviously the perfume from aloes was expensive, considering its source. No doubt only the rich could afford the luxury of its use. Such a man was Nicodemus who came to the tomb of Jesus bringing a hundred-pound weight of myrrh and aloes for use in preparing his body for burial. Said John: "Then took they the body of Jesus, and wound it in linen clothes with the spices, as the manner of the Jews is to bury" (John 19:39, 40).

Amber

Amber is not a tree. Rather, it is a fossil resin from the now extinct pine tree, *Pinus succinifera*. This pine once grew along the former shores of the Baltic Sea in the Eocene period *(Fig. 3–1)*, said by geologists to be over 50 million years ago. It was not, however, restricted to this area alone since amber has since been found in other parts of the world.

Amber is a very hard but brittle substance, ranging in color from transparent to almost opaque. Its color varies, from yellowish and brownish, to blackish. Amber takes on a high polish when rubbed and gives off an aromatic odor. It can be processed to produce an oil.

The prophet Ezekiel refers to its color in his vision. Said he: "And I looked, and, behold, a whirlwind came out of the north, a great cloud, and a fire infolding itself, and a brightness was about it, and out of the midst thereof as the color of amber, out of the midst of the fire "(Ezek. 1:4).

Amber was brought overland from the shores of the Baltic to the Danube to provide pomp and delicacy for Rome.

It was highly prized by the Romans and Greeks for beads and other ornamental purposes and for carvings. No doubt it was used for similar purposes during the early biblical period. In A.D. 77 amber was first recognized as a product of the plant world.

It is interesting to note that amber has been found with ancient insects and plants trapped therein. Some insects and spiders have been so well preserved that the muscle tissues and fine hairs may be studied under a microscope by scientists.

Apple

Upon mention of apple, *Pyrus malus*, a biblical reader will immediately think of Adam and Eve in the Garden of Eden. Yet, nowhere in the creation story is an apple referred to. It was an unknown fruit tree in the midst of the garden from which Eve plucked the fruit, the Tree of Knowledge (Gen. 3:3–6).

The prevailing view of the apple being in the Garden of Eden is thought to stem from a misinterpretation of Song of Solomon 8:5. Biblical authorities agree that "apple" is not so intended by this passage.

One school of thought says that the apple was originally native to Asia Minor and was distributed by the Hittite traders throughout the holy lands. Others say that apples were too primitive in the Mesopotamian valley for table consumption, if indeed they ever grew there. Yet, the majority view is that apples did grow in the region. It is known that Neolithic man in Europe ate crabapples and may have cultivated wild forms.

It is evident from tables unearthed in the ruins of San that orchards of apples, pomegranates, olives, and figs were growing in Egypt (1301–1234 B.C.) when the Israelites were making bricks for the treasure cities (Exod. 1:8–11). This was before the Exodus from Egypt by Moses about 1290 B.C. It is known that the Egyptians prepared cider from apples.

Biblical references make it appear evident that the scriptural writers knew what they were speaking of and not some other fruit. They referred to the smell of the apple (Song of Sol. 7:8), its sweetness (Song of Sol. 2:3), and its use for revival of themselves when faint (Song of Sol. 2:5). An allusion is also made to its size (Song of Sol. 8:5).

The Romans had knowledge of over twenty varieties of apples.

Some say "the apple of the Garden of Eden" was a golden apricot, *Prunus armenica,* since the biblical description would equally apply to this fruit. There are those who also say that the apple of Joel's withering prophecy was an apricot (Joel 1:12).

Apricot

The apricot, *Prunus armenica,* is indigenous to Armenia and is today an abundant fruit in Palestine, second to figs. It became adapted to Cyprus where it is known as the "golden apple."

The apricot was cultivated in China as early as 2000 B.C. A substitute for almond oil is obtained from its seeds.

Some authorities consider apricot as being the fruit tree in the Garden of Eden. However, the uncertainty of its origin has raised questions as to this view.

Ash

The name "ash" occurs but once in the King James Version of the Bible. There is general agreement that the true ash, *Fraxinus sp.,* was not intended. What tree was referred to by the original Hebrew word "oren" is unknown. Some Bibles refer to the genus "pine" rather than "ash" in the translation.

There are three pines common to Syria, including the maritime pine, *Pinus pinea,* widely used in plantings. One authority speculates that maritime pine may have been the species intended since the wood is hard enough to be carved into an image (Isa. 14:14, 15).

There are three species of ash common to Lebanon, and

these could have been part of the forest stands in the original mountain forests of Bible lands. These are *F. ornus, F. parvifolia,* and *F. syriaca.* However, it is evident that ash was not specifically referred to in biblical passages.

Aspen

The aspen, *Populus euphratica,* with its drooping leaves is considered by some authorities as the "willows" on which discouraged Hebrew exiles hung their harps as they sat by the river of Babylon and wept, with no heart to sing songs of Zion in a strange land (Ps. 137:1, 2).

Some individuals are of the opinion that the weeping willow, *Salix Babylonica,* was the tree upon which the Hebrews hung their harps. Biblical authorities and botanists do not agree. The weeping willow is a native of China and is not thought to have been introduced in Babylon during Old Testament times. There is no evidence of its presence during the biblical period.

Aspen, otherwise known as Euphrates poplar, was extensively used as a building material during the period of King Solomon.

Balm of Gilead

Balm of Gilead is the balm produced from the sap or gum of the trees *Balsamodendron gileadense* and *B. opobalsamum* indigenous to southern Arabia. In Roman times, and perhaps earlier, it was cultivated in the lower Jordan Valley, thus being near Gilead from which its name was derived.

In commerce, the balm went by the name of "Balm of Gilead," and in early years was an important ingredient in medicine. It has since fallen into disuse. In trade today it is known as "Mecca balsam."

During the early Bible period, Gilead was a trade center for the balm. The balm was probably produced at or near Gilead, or was a prime article of commerce from this point. Josephus reported that balsam was growing in Palestine since the time of King Solomon, being cultivated principally near Jericho. The plants were probably grown from seed given to Solomon by the Queen of Sheba as a gift.

Discussing the area near Jericho, Josephus said: "Wherein is such plenty of trees produced as are very rare, and of the most excellent sort. It also bears the balsam which is the most precious of all the fruits in that place, cypress trees also, and those that bear myrobalanum."

It is known that Roman soldiers found balsam trees growing near Jericho and sent branches of these to Rome as a sign of victory over the Jews. One thousand years later the Crusaders found no trace of the trees. No doubt the Turks, in their control of the land, neglected to care for them and they died.

Mention of the balm for medicinal purposes is found in the Scriptures (Jer. 8:22; 46:11; 51:8) and was widely used during this period of history.

That the balm was an article of commerce much in demand in Egypt is shown by the Ishmaelites who, in a camel caravan, were carrying "spicery and balm and myrrh" to Egypt (Gen. 37:25). It was to these Ishmaelites that the sons of Jacob sold their brother Joseph into slavery.

Evidently Jacob was knowledgeable about balm since he sent a small amount of this substance, with honey, spices, myrrh, nuts, and almonds to Egypt by his sons (Gen. 43:11).

Both Israel and Judaea dealt in balm during the latter days of the monarchies (Ezek. 27:17). In the Talmud, it is said that eighty pounds of opobalsamum was used at the funeral of a rabbi.

In early Greece the rich put balsam in water, mingled with wine, to render it additionally fragrant in the washing of feet before a banquet.

Today the monks of Jericho produce a so-called "Balm of Gilead" from the fruits of *Balanites aegyptiaca* which they claim has healing power. Authorities agree that this substance has no claim to being the original balm of the Bible.

Balsam

The balsam tree produced the balm known as "Balm of Gilead." Refer to the discussion under "Balm of Gilead."

Balsam did not grow naturally in Bible lands, but rather in South Arabia. Some authorities say the mulberry of 2 Samuel 5:23, 24 and 1 Chronicles 14:14, 15 may be balsam, but there is much disagreement on this point.

One biblical writer speculates that Bacca of Psalm 84:6 refers to the balsam trees formerly growing in the Valley of Rephaim (2 Sam. 5:22, 23, R.V.). Balsam trees exude a tear-like gum.

This balsam tree is in no way related to the balsam fir, *Abies balsamea,* of the United States.

Bay

The "green bay tree" was David's symbol of wicked people who appear prosperous and influential. Said David: "I have seen the wicked in great power, and spreading himself like a green bay tree" (Ps. 37:35).

Was the green bay intended, however? Biblical scholars seem to be in accord that the translation of the passage should be "a green tree that groweth in his own soil." The Revised Standard Version refers to "cedar" in this passage.

There is a bay tree in biblical lands known scientifically as *Lauris nobilis (Fig. 6–7),* an evergreen laurel. Its aro-

Fig. 6–7. Leaves of the green bay tree. King David used the tree, in one biblical version, as a symbol of wicked people who appear prosperous and influential. SL

matic leaves are used to flavor food, and its roots and bark are used for medicinal purposes.

This bay tree is native to the Mediterranean area and is one of the world's oldest flavoring ingredients. Both whole and crushed leaves are imported into the United States from Turkey, Greece, Yugoslavia, and Portugal. Bay is indispensable in pickling and in the manufacture of vinegars.

Wreaths of bay leaves were used by the Greeks and Romans to crown their heroes. One record shows that when the Greeks began the Olympic games in 1453 B.C., the victors were awarded bay leaf wreaths.

Bay is known to have been planted in the ancient gardens of Tyre and Sidon, and was considered by some an emblem of wealth.

Bdellium

Bdellium is the first aromatic substance referred to in the Bible. It is reported in Genesis 2:12 in reference to the land of Havilah: "And the gold of that land is good: there is bdellium and the onyx stone."

Bdellium is a fragrant resinous gum from a tree shrub, *Commiphora mukul,* which grew in arid regions of western India. Some authorities say it also grew in Arabia. Incisions made in the bark of the tree produced a gum which hardened into waxlike translucent pellets. Early Egyptian women carried these in pouches as perfume.

Josephus compares manna to Bdellium "in sweetness and pleasant taste." The Bible says it had the same color as manna (Num. 11:7).

Bdellium was reportedly sold as a cheap aromatic substitute for myrrh.

Beech

Though not reported in the Bible, it is known from jewelry boxes found in biblical Ur in southern Babylonia, the Sumer of ancient times, that beech trees, *Fagus sp.,* were growing in this area in the third millennium B.C. *(Fig. 6–8).*

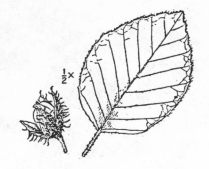

Fig. 6–8. Drawing of the leaf and fruit of the European beech, *Fagus sylvatica*. Evidence strongly suggests that this tree once grew in biblical Ur, in southern Babylonia. USFS

Excavations of the tomb of the Sumerian Queen Shub-ad who lived about 5000 B.C. revealed a crown of gold on which artists had engraved beech leaves.

It can be speculated that, in ancient times, the flood plain area of the Euphrates and Tigris rivers once supported a dense stand of various tree species, among which was beech. It may well be that Noah used timber from this area to build the ark.

Box

The box tree was mentioned twice by Isaiah (Isa. 41:19; 60:13). Yet, there is no reliable information as to the tree intended from the original Hebrew word.

While there is a Syrian box tree, *Buxus longifolia,* in northern Palestine, Lebanon, and Syria, it ranges in size from a shrub to a small tree. Under good growing conditions it rarely exceeds a height of twenty feet.

One authority states that it is unlikely such a small tree would be associated with familiar trees like cedar, shittah, pine, fir, and myrtle (Isa. 60:13). There is no universal agreement on this, however.

An old Arab view is that the wild cypress or lizzab, *Juniperous excelsa,* might be the tree to which Isaiah had reference.

Carob

The wild carob tree, *Ceratonia siliqua,* produces long pods of sweet pulp called St. John's-bread. Other common names given to the fruit are "locust bean" and "locust." In Spain it is known as Algaroba and in Arabia as Bharoat. An evergreen cultivated throughout the Bible land but considered a native of Syria and Palestine, it is one of the most common trees native to Palestine.

Fig. 6–9. The carob tree is well known for the fruit it produces. Its husks, or fruit pods, have been used throughout history as food for animal and man. It was the food of the prodigal son. SL

The carob is associated with the prodigal son who ended up feeding pigs, and who in hunger ate the husks *(Fig. 6–9)* the swine were feeding upon (Luke 15:16). The husks to which the Scripture refers have long been associated with the carob fruit.

While carob pods were fed to swine because of their availability and nutritive value, they were and still are used as food by many people. Today they are widely used as fodder for cattle and sheep as well as hogs. The pods are said by some to have been the food of John the Baptist (Matt. 3:4).

Some Arabs hold the view that the carob tree contains evil spirits, and they consider it unsafe to sit under its branches.

The carob is a small tree, generally ten to twenty feet high with glossy green foliage, preferring rocky, dry soils on which to grow. It is very productive of fruit. The seeds within the pods are stony.

Dried carob pods are about four to eight inches long and contain about 50 percent sugar. In biblical cities they were sold to be eaten like candy. The pods are also ground and the substance used as a food supplement throughout the world. The Arabs today prepare a syrupy preparation from the pods. Food faddists use flour from the ground-up pods as a substitute for chocolate because of its low fat content. *Johannisbrod*, esteemed by some in Germany, is made from the pulp of this pod.

This tree is grown today as an ornamental in the subtropical regions of the United States.

Some authorities say that certain passages of the Old Testament referring to "honey" had reference to carob.

The seeds of the carob pod were once used by jewelers as the carat weight.

Cassia

Cassia is an evergreen tree of the *Cinnamomum* family, known scientifically as *Cinnamomum cassia*. It is a native of China, Indo-China, and Indonesia.

From both the dried bark and buds of the cassia are derived the spices and oils that have been products of commerce for centuries. The buds in particular have a high oil content and have the same flavor and aroma as cinnamon bark. As an article of commerce it came across the Indian Ocean in trade between the people. From this point it came across Arabia and thence by caravan to the Mediterranean countries.

Moses was knowledgeable about cassia and cinnamon and used both, along with other ingredients, to make the holy anointing oil "after the art of the apothecary" (Exod. 30:23–25).

Cassia was used in the time of the Hebrews to scent clothing (Ps. 45:8). It was also traded in the market at Tyre (Ezek. 27:19).

Evidence that cassia and cinnamon were extensively used in Temple worship by the Hebrews was reported by Josephus. He stated that when Titus was in the act of demolishing the walls of Jerusalem a man named Phineas, a deserter, showed Titus a large quantity of cinnamon and cassia. These, with other sweet spices, had been placed in storage. They were "mixed together and offered as incense to God every day."

Fig. 6–10. Cassia and cinnamon are most generally sold today in bark form. Peeled from the trees, the bark is formed in hollow tubes and dried.

Cassia is inferior to cinnamon. In both, the product is the bark peeled from the branches and stems of trees in the form of hollow tubes which are dried *(Fig. 6–10).*

During the period of Herodotus, it was the current belief, spread perhaps by cassia and cinnamon merchants, that cassia grew in a shallow lake around which lodged fierce winged bats. These made a horrible screeching sound. To secure the cassia, Arabians covered themselves with hides so they could reach the trees.

Refer to comments under "cinnamon."

Cedar of Lebanon

The cedar of Lebanon, *Cedrus libani,* *(Fig. 4–2)* is perhaps one of the most beloved trees in the Bible. It is mentioned some seventy times. While it is closely associated with Lebanon, its range extends from the Himalayas to the Atlas, and from Central Asia Minor to Lebanon. It was once abundant in Amanus and the Taurus. Extensive forests once were present on the island of Cyprus, and at one period of history Cyprus was a wholesale market for the wood product. At Bersherri, in Lebanon, there is today a sacred remnant of the original forest area. It is called "The Cedars of the Lord" *(Fig. 3–14).*

While most references to cedar in the Bible aptly refer to the "cedar of Lebanon" there are, according to authorities, a few exceptions. The cedar wood used by Moses in the ritual of purification (Lev. 14:4–6; Num. 19:6) is thought by some to be a juniper plant native to the Sinai desert, such as *Juniperus phoenica.* Juniper is found in Mount Hor and vicinity, and in the mountains of Sinai. Opinion has been expressed that, in this period of history, wood from the cedars of Lebanon would have been difficult to obtain.

There is also the question as to the "cedar trees beside the water" (Num. 24:6). The cedar tree never did grow naturally on this site and the reference is thought to pertain to another species no longer in existence.

As pointed out in the Bible, the cedar of Lebanon was a tall tree (Isa. 2:13), its chief habitat being Lebanon (Judg. 9:15). It was a tree with fair branches, having a shadowing shroud *(Fig. 6–11)*, and a crown that was in the top of the forest canopy (Ezek. 31:8). Masts for ships were made from boles of the trees (Ezek. 27:5) and from the wood were made pillars, beams, and boards (1 Kings 6:9; 7:2). The wood was also used for carving (Isa. 44:14). Its cones are a thing of beauty (see inset, p. 97).

The lofty branches of the tree provided a nesting place for storks (Ezek. 31:6). The merchants of Tyre sold "chests of rich apparel, bound with cords, and made of cedar" (Ezek. 27:24). The cedar tree was considered by Solomon as a symbol of grandeur and might (Ps. 92:12).

A scribe, Hori, officer of the royal stables under Ramesses II, had this to say of the forests of Lebanon: "Lebanon, where the sky is dark in broad daylight. It is overgrown with cypresses, oaks and cedars which rise sky high."

The cedar of Lebanon is most noted as the contribution of timber by Hiram, King of Tyre (1 Kings 5:6–10; 9:11), to King David to build his palace (2 Sam. 5:11; 1 Chron. 17:1) and to King Solomon for use in the temple construction, as well as Solomon's house and other important buildings in Jerusalem (2 Sam. 5:11; 1 Chron. 17:1; 1 Kings 5:6–10; 9:11; Ezra 3:7).

Cedar wood from the forests of Lebanon is also known to have been used for roofing the temple of Diana at Ephesus, that of Apollo at Utica, and other famous structures such as the great hall of the palace of Xerxes. It was also used to build fleets of ships for trade and for Egyptian solar boats to carry the pharaohs' souls.

Chestnut

Contrary to biblical references (Gen. 30:37; Ezek. 31:8) the chestnut tree, *Castanea sp.*, is not considered by biblical authorities to be the one intended. Rather, they say, it is more likely to be the plane tree, *Platanus sp.* It is so referred to in the Living Bible, the Jerusalem Bible, and the Revised Standard Version. The principal reason is that a scratch in the bark of a plane tree would produce a "white streak." Such would not be the case with chestnut.

Chestnut is found, however, in biblical lands, but it is a rare species.

Jacob took fresh shoots from the poplar, almond, and plane trees, and peeled white streaks in them. These he placed beside the watering troughs. When his flock mated before these shoots, their offspring were streaked and spotted. All three trees mentioned would produce a whitish streak when peeled.

The plane tree grows to a great height and has an imposing appearance. This would accommodate the comparison of this tree with the cedar of Lebanon as made in Ezekiel 31:8.

The plane tree is abundant along the water courses of Syria and in Mesopotamia.

The Americanized name for plane tree is "sycamore."
See discussion under "plane tree."

Fig. 6–11. A large, 150-year-old cedar of Lebanon in Geneva, Switzerland. It was planted from seed in 1735. The picture was taken in 1885 by Gifford Pinchot, outstanding forest conservationist. Note shadowing shroud referred to in biblical passages. USFS, USDA *Inset:* what appears to be a rose is, in reality, the top portion of a cedar of Lebanon cone. The lower part of the cone was stripped away (photo courtesy Malcom Moore).

Cinnamon

From the beginning of recorded history man has used cinnamon, *Cinnamomum zeylanicum,* and there is no dispute among biblical authorities as to the substance intended by Bible references. *(Fig. 6–12a).*

Imported from the East, it was used by the Hebrews as an ingredient in the holy anointing oil (Exod. 30:23), for perfuming beds (Prov. 7:16, 17), and apparently was cultivated by Solomon (Song of Sol. 4:14). It was also a part of the wares of Babylon the Great (Rev. 18:13).

Cinnamon is the dried bark of a species in the plant genus *Cinnamomum,* of the family *Lauraceae (Fig. 6–12b).* Today several species of cinnamon are grown commercially in many parts of the world.

From the leaves of the cinnamon tree, an "oil of cinnamon leaf" is extracted. It is better known in the trade as "clove oil" which it resembles in odor. Fragrant oil is also derived from the fruit and bark.

It is interesting to note that, in A.D. 65, the funeral rites for Nero's wife Poppaea, at Rome, consumed a year's cinnamon supply.

During his travels, Herodotus heard of the reported means used to collect cinnamon. Presumably, large birds carried rolls of cinnamon to their rocky and inaccessible nests. To obtain these rolls, Arabians placed large pieces of meat on the ground near the trees. The birds carried the meat to their nests. The weight of the meat caused the nests to fall down. Whereupon the cinnamon was collected. Apparently, this rumor was spread by those engaged in commerce. At any rate, the story seems to have been accepted in that period.

In 1656 cinnamon was made a state monopoly in Ceylon by the Dutch. *Cinnamomum zeylanicum* is the species indigenous to this country. It is more popular in other parts of the world than in the United States.

Like cassia, the product of cinnamon is peeled from the

Fig 6–12a. A young cinnamon tree growing in India. Although cinnamon was used extensively during the biblical period, it was not native to Bible lands. Moses used cinnamon as one of the ingredients in the holy anointing oil. BPS

Fig. 6–12b. Harvesting cinnamon bark in Indonesia. As early as the time of Moses, cinnamon bark was a well-known item of commerce throughout the known world (photo courtesy American Spice Trade Association).

branches in hollow tubes as seen in grocery stores (Fig. 6–10).

Citron

Citron, *Citrus medica*, (Fig. 6–13), was one of the "goodly trees" in Bible times (Lev. 23:40). The fruit was used largely in salads, and the fine wood was esteemed by craftsmen.

There are several varieties of the fruit, including the lime, lemon, and bergamot. Bergamot is inedible but highly fragrant.

The dried flowers, leaves, and oils derived from them were employed in perfumes, flavored drinks, and for other uses by the apothecaries of the period.

Citron was planted in the Hanging Gardens of Babylon. It was used by the Babylonians for toilet water and pomades, among other things. The citron, otherwise known as Etrog, has one botanical feature found in no other fruit in that the female part of the flower remains attached to the ripened fruit.

Cottonwood

Refer to discussion under "aspen."

Cypress

Cypress, *Cupressus sempervirens, var. horizontalis,* was originally an important species in the mountains of ancient Palestine. That it grew "high among the clouds" is shown in the Apocryphal Book of Ecclesiasticus (50:10). Cypress also grew wild in Gilead and Edom. It is native to the eastern Mediterranean countries (Fig. 6–14).

Because of the nature of the wood and its durability it was extensively used in the construction of ships. It was also used to make idols of worship (Isa. 44:15). Some say that the cypress referred to by Isaiah was the variety *pyramidalis*. Others say it was not "cypress" to which Isaiah had reference, but rather it was an evergreen oak.

. 6–13. Preparing the Etrog or citron for
pment to Jewish communities for Suc-
h, or the Feast of Tabernacles. The citron
one of the "goodly trees" of the biblical
riod. CGI/Fig. 6–14. Cypress trees grow-
around a church near Cana in northern
el. They are extensively used as orna-
ntals today. In size, these trees cannot be
npared to those in the original forest.

Still others say it was a "holm oak," *Quercus ilex,* as shown in the Vulgate.

Cypress was an important timber tree during the early biblical period. It is considered to be the tree from which Noah obtained wood to build the ark. The doors of St. Peter's church in Rome were made of cypress wood and are over one thousand years old.

Cypress was also extensively used as a building material.

Scattered isolated cypress are still found in the mountains of Gilead, Edom, and Sinai.

In Israel, cypress is used largely today as an ornamental tree and for use in windbreaks in orange groves.

Date Palm

While there are several palms native to Bible lands, the use of "palm" in the Scriptures usually designates the palm tree, *Phoenix dactylifera.* Referred to more than sixty times, it is the tree that produces the most welcome fruit of the Bible. It is believed by some individuals that the date palm may have been the "Tree of Life" in the Garden of Eden.

Pliny reports that more than forty-nine varieties of dates were grown in the Jordan Valley during his period. Josephus refers to "many sorts of palm trees, different from each other in taste and name; the better sort of them, when they are pressed, yield an excellent kind of honey, not much inferior in sweetness to other honey."

As a tree, the date palm *(Fig. 6–15)* often reaches a height of eighty feet, particularly on productive soils with adequate moisture. While it has much ornamental and economic value, it was and is most useful for food. The tree is dioecious, that is, there are both male and female trees, and it is propagated by seeds or cuttings.

The date palm was grown in ancient Egypt and the fruit it bears, in tints of gold, mahogany, and yellow, have been enjoyed by the people of the Holy Land for centuries. It is a prolific fruit producer.

Fig. 6–15. Date palms growing near El-Arish in the Gaza strip. Mediterranean Sea is in background. SL

The fruit is highly edible and nourishing and has a natural sugar content of about 50 percent. The seed can be ground up and used as food for camels. Josephus speaks of a syrup made from the dates.

The sap of the tree yields a sugar from which a strong drink called "arrack" is made. Leaves were used to cover roofs, to build fences and to make baskets, mats, and other household items. Wax, tannin, dye stuffs, and oil have also been obtained from the tree. The trunk of the tree supplied timber. Robes were woven from the fibers of the leaves.

The alluvial plains of the Mesopotamia area have always favored date production. Ancient clay tablets found in excavations show that date palm groves were used for barter.

Normally, palm trees live up to a century or more. They have long tap roots that seek out water. Their presence in almost desertlike conditions is indicative of the availability of water (Exod. 15:27). Growing under these conditions, the palm is a fitting symbol of prosperity, uprightness, patience, and constancy as ascribed to it by Bible passages.

Fig. 6–16. The Bible refers to Jericho as the city of palm trees. Today, palm trees are still in abundance throughout the city and its environs.

By Christian times, the palm came to denote victory (Rev. 7:9) and became a symbol of triumph (John 12:13).

In the area of Jericho, and along the banks of the Jordan, grew the best date palms. Jericho was known as "the city of palm trees" (Deut. 34:3). See *Fig. 6–16.*

While Jericho today is a city of palm trees, such has not always been the case. In 1833 an authority stated that but one palm tree survived. In 1866 it was reported that "the last palm has gone from the plain which once gave Jericho the name of the city of date palms." This included Ein Gedi which was once a forest of palm trees.

Palms were characterized by the early Hebrews as "goodly trees" and the leaves were used to celebrate the Feast of Tabernacles (Lev. 23:40; Neh. 8:15). In art, the palm formed a motif for King Solomon's Temple (1 Kings 6:29; 2 Chron. 3:5). To the psalmist the beauty and utility of palm was related to the godly (Ps. 92:12).

It was under a palm tree that Deborah, a prophetess, dwelt and "the children of Israel came up to her for judgment" (Judg. 4:5). Ezekiel's vision of the future temple included the palm in its design.

During the wanderings of the Israelites, they came to Elim where there were "threescore and ten palm trees; and they pitched there" (Num. 33:9).

It is of historical interest to note that Darius the Great used as his seal a depiction of a two-wheeled chariot between two date palms. This is an indication of the importance he attached to the palm tree.

When Jesus was making his triumphal entry into Jerusalem on the first Palm Sunday, it was the branches of palm that were waved and spread before him (John 12:13).

Ebony

Several species of trees provide the wood known as ebony. It has been an article of commerce since ancient times. Ebony was brought to Palestine from Dedon on the Persian Gulf (Ezek. 27:15) and from Ethiopia. There is a

Fig. 6–17. Ebony tree. The wood from this species was extensively used for furniture by the Phoenicians and Babylonians. It has been speculated that much of the wood used during the biblical period came from India. BPS

lack of information as to the exact species from which the wood was obtained in Ethiopia. It is possible that ebony from India was also used in biblical lands.

Ebony, indigenous to the East Indies and extensively traded in commerce, is known scientifically as *Diospyros ebenum (Fig. 6–17),* a relative of the common persimmon found in the United States.

Some authorities say that ebony from the East Indies was the tree from which wood was obtained and referred to by biblical writers.

Ebony is a hard, close-grained wood. The heartwood of the tree is blackish in color. Hard and heavy, the wood has a fine grain. It takes a high polish.

The Phoenicians, Greeks, and Babylonians prized ebony for use in furniture, some of which had ivory inlaid in the wood. It was also used to make household vessels. Ebony was also known in Egypt, and pieces of it have been found in old Egyptian tombs. It was a part of Tyre's trade with the "men of Rhodes" (Ezek. 27:15).

Elm

In Hosea's condemnation of the people of Israel for their sins, he related to them their disobedience to God for making sacrifices to idols on the top of the mountains. He also criticized them for burning incense under the oaks, poplars, and elms (Hos. 4:13). This reference to elm, *Ulmus sp.,* is the only one in the Bible.

There is agreement among biblical scholars that the original Hebrew word more aptly describes the terebinth or pistacia tree than the elm. "Terebinth" is the word used instead of "elm" in the Revised Standard Version, the Jerusalem Bible, and the Living Bible.

Fig

From the beginning of recorded history the fig, *Ficus carica,* has played an important role in the life of the people. It was a favorite staple food, either as a fresh fruit or in dried condition. In the latter form it was a major item of commerce. The fig is mentioned over sixty times in the Bible. As a tree, the fig was valued for its heavy shade.

In Egypt, which was always short of trees, the fig was valued for its shade, fruit, and the wood which the trees provided. Ancient Egyptians used the wood for household utensils, boxes, coffins, and especially for construction purposes.

From Talmudic literature it is evident that in Egypt, the fig was more valued for its wood than its fruit, although the latter was of importance. It was extensively planted for its stout beams which were used for construction purposes. The remains of wood, roots, and fruit discovered in Egypt date back as far as the predynastic period, more than 3000 B.C.

In biblical times failure of a fig crop was considered a national calamity, while productiveness was taken as a token of peace and divine favor.

Helena, queen of Adiabene, is remembered by the people of Judaea for her contribution of figs to a starving nation, in a famine foretold by the prophet Agabus (Acts 11:28). Helena was the mother of King Izates. She had accepted the Jewish religion and become zealous in the faith. When the famine arrived she sent some of her servants to Alexandria to buy grain, and others to Cyprus to bring a large cargo of dried figs. These she distributed to those in want throughout Judaea and became renowned for her charitable contribution.

Figs are generally associated with the palm, vine, and pomegranate in the Bible. They were common in Egypt (Ps. 105:33).

The fig differs from most fruits in that it is greenish, inconspicuous, and concealed among the leaves until the period of ripening *(Fig. 6–18)*. Little recognized by the average person is the fact that the fruit is really a bud with the flowers inside.

Jesus came upon a fig tree when he was hungry and "he

found nothing thereon, but leaves only, and said unto it, Let no fruit grow on thee henceforth for ever. And presently the fig withered away" (Matt. 21:18, 19). It was this tree that Christ cursed.

Two varieties of figs were common to Palestine. One was an early season producer, the other a later one. The first produced a larger, more juicy fruit and was eaten fresh. The late figs were generally dried and pressed into cakes for future use, or for the market (1 Sam. 25:18). The island of Chios, which in Paul's time was part of Rome, was famous for its figs.

Figs were used for medicinal purposes. It was Hezekiah, "sick unto death" with a boil, who was cured with Isaiah's prescription of a "lump of figs" (2 Kings 20:1, 7).

In the Bible the fig is used as a symbol of prosperity and plenty (1 Kings 4:25; Micah 4:4). Nathanael was under a fig tree when Jesus saw him (John 1:48–50) and recognized qualities of discipleship in this one "in whom there is no guile" (John 1:47–50).

Christ used the fig tree in two of his parables: once as indicative of summer when the tree has tender branches that put forth leaves, and the other to give the fig tree an additional year beyond three, with special attention and fertilizer, to produce fruit (Matt. 24:32; Luke 13:6–9).

Figs and pomegranates were fruits brought back to Moses by the spies whom he had sent out to the Promised Land (Num. 13:2, 3).

Bethphage, a village on the Mount of Olives, was named after a fig tree. It means "house of unripe figs."

Large palmate fig leaves provided the covering for Adam and Eve (Gen. 3:7).

Fir

The fir tree is referred to in many passages in the Bible, yet there is no agreement among authorities as to the real species intended from the Hebrew word. Some favor cy-

Fig. 6–18. Figs differ from other fruits in that they are greenish, inconspicuous, and concealed among the leaves until the period of ripening. TFS

press, *Cupressus sempervirens,* since it is native to the Bible lands. Others say that the references may have been to pine, *Pinus halpensis,* or juniper, *Juniperus excelsa,* which are also native to the region. While the weight of authority seems to favor the juniper, the true fir, *Abies cilicica,* does grow in high alpine regions like the cedar of Lebanon. Because of the sparsity of the species biblical authorities seem to question the fir.

In biblical references it is shown that fir was used for musical instruments (2 Sam. 6:5); that it was given by Hiram of Tyre to Solomon and used in building the Temple (1 Kings 5:8, 10; 6:15, 34; 2 Chron. 3:5); used for rafters (Song of Sol. 1:17); and for ships (Ezek. 27:5). It was also a tree in which storks built their nests in the mountainous areas (Ps. 104:17).

The true fir, as referred to in the Bible, has the wood characteristics that would enable it to serve the purposes cited by the various passages.

Frankincense

Frankincense or alibanum as referred to in the Scriptures is a gum resin from a tree *(Fig. 6–19a and 6–19b).*

There is no "frankincense tree" per se. However, most authorities believe that frankincense was obtained from the tree, *Boswellia carteri,* and related Asiatic and African species.

When a deep incision is made in this tree, a yellowish milky juice is produced. In about three months it dries into a resin known as frankincense.

There are many biblical references to frankincense. It was the perfume placed before the Tabernacle (Exod. 30:34–36), placed on meat offerings (Lev. 2:1, 2), and recognized as a sweet smelling perfume (Song of Sol. 3:6).

Perhaps it is best known as one of the precious gifts presented to Christ at his birth, along with gold and myrrh, by the wise men (Matt. 2:11).

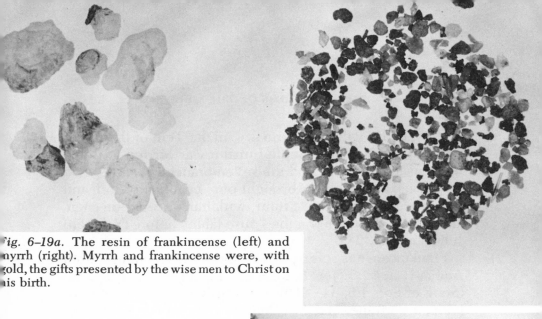

Fig. 6–19a. The resin of frankincense (left) and myrrh (right). Myrrh and frankincense were, with gold, the gifts presented by the wise men to Christ on his birth.

Fig. 6–19b. A tree, *Boswellia serrata*, from which the gum resin frankincense is obtained. When an incision is made in the trunk, a yellowish milky juice is produced. In about three months it dries into a resin known as frankincense. BPS

Outside the Vale of Testimony, in the Tent of the Meeting, and later in the Temple (until it was carried to Rome by Titus in A.D. 70), stood the seven-branched candlestick. To it, each Sabbath, was brought pure beaten olive oil, and twelve cakes of the finest flour, with frankincense on each, and placed in rows upon the "pure table" before (Yahweh) Jehovah (Lev. 24:6).

Frankincense is referred to in the Bible as coming from Arabia (Isa. 60:6; Jer. 6:20) and probably from Palestine (Song of Sol. 4:6, 14). It was extensively used as a medicine, a perfume, and in religious rites by the Egyptians and Hebrews.

In the Zadokite Document of the Dead Sea Scrolls there is a rule for the Sabbath. It states, "No one is to wear soiled clothes, or clothes that have been put in storage unless they be first laundered and rubbed with frankincense."

The extensive use of frankincense is pointed out in the history of Herodotus. He reports that each year "the Arabians of the far south sent 25 tons of frankincense" to Darius, the great Persian King (523–447 B.C.). In this period of history the kingdom of Darius was divided into twenty satrapies. From each he demanded tribute annually. While the "Arabians from the far south" were not in his kingdom, they felt obligated to pay him for protection, as did others beyond his frontiers.

The Egyptians used frankincense for embalming and fumigating.

Galbanum

The galbanum of the Bible is a gum resin or gum with a pungent odor that was used, in part, to make the perfume or holy ointment for use in the Tabernacle of the Congregation (Exod. 30:34–36).

It is believed to have been derived from two species of woody shrubs, *Ferula galbaniflua* and *F. rubricaulis,* both native to Persia.

The gum was and is still used in medicine as an anti-spasmodic. It is characterized as a greasy, sticky, granulated gum of whitish appearance when first extracted from the tree, but afterward turning yellowish. The gum has a pungent odor and taste. When mixed with fragrant substances it has the effect of increasing the odor and fixing it longer.

The Hebrew word for galbanum is "whiteness."

Galbanum is said by one authority to have been the frankincense presented to Christ at his birth (Matt. 2:11). However, this is not the opinion held by the majority. See comments under "frankincense."

Gopher Wood

And God said unto Noah, "Make thee an ark of gopher wood; rooms shalt thou make in the ark, and shall pitch it within and without with pitch . . . . This did Noah; according to all that God commanded him, so he did" (Gen. 6:14, 22).

As previously stated, the tree which provided the wood from which the ark was constructed is unknown. Most biblical authorities express the view that it was probably some resinous wood, such as pine, cedar or cypress.

The weight of opinion favors cypress, *Cupressus sempervirens, var horizontalis,* since this species was widely used in boat construction by the merchant people of the eastern Mediterranean, from Greece to Phoenicia.

Only if Noah's ark is ever uncovered under the snows of Mt. Ararat will we be in a position to know with certainty what species Noah used.

Exploring Mt. Ararat in 1969, Fernard Navarra did locate a piece of wood thought to be a part of the ark. It was oak, *Quercus sp.* There has been no general acceptance of this.

Further information on the ark is presented in Chapter 15.

Hazel

The Bible tells of Jacob taking sprigs of green poplar, hazel, and chestnut trees and peeling white streaks in them (Gen. 30:37).

As in the case of the chestnut, the prevailing view is that the Hebrew was misinterpreted. Rather than being "hazel," *Corylus sp.*, it is said it should be "almond." See comments under "chestnut" and "poplar."

The Living Bible refers to the tree as "almond."

Henna

Henna is a small tree, *Lawsonia inermis (Fig. 6–20a)*, native to Egypt, Arabia, India, and Persia. From its yellow flowers, leaves, and young shoots a dye is obtained *(Fig. 20b)*. The dye ranges from an orange to a yellowish red.

Fig. 6–20a. A henna tree. This species was cultivated as a garden crop in biblical times. BPS

Fig. 6–20b. Close-up view of the henna tree. From this tree the henna dye is produced, as it has been for centuries. Its use for dyeing purposes was well known throughout the biblical period. *Inset:* a close-up of the fruit. SL

The dye produced from henna is known as a very fast dye. For centuries it has been used (and is still used today) for dyeing hair, toes, eyebrows, fingernails, and for other personal adornment.

In some parts of the world today the leaves of the plant are powdered. This powder is then made into a paste with water and applied to the hair. It is allowed to remain in the hair overnight before washing. The resulting hair color is reddish-brown.

Presumably the yellow flowers were first used to produce the famous dyestuff.

In biblical times henna was cultivated as a garden crop.

The "camphire" of Song of Solomon (1:4; 4:13) is said to be "henna."

Henna has also been referred to as the "loosestrife bush."

Hemlock

There are only two references to hemlock in the King James Version of the Bible.

In the eighth century B.C. the prophet Hosea, condemning the sinful nature of Israel, said: "They have spoken words, swearing falsely in making a covenant; thus judgment springeth up as a hemlock in the furrows of the field" (Hos. 10:4).

Amos, a later prophet of about 750 B.C., said: "Shall horses run upon the rock? Will one plow there with oxen? For ye have turned judgment into gall, and the fruit of righteousness into hemlock" (Amos 6:12).

There is agreement that the references to hemlock, *Tsuga sp.*, were unfortunate translations of the original Hebrew. Authorities hold to the view that Hosea had reference to a plant, but the genera or species to which he referred is unknown. One says "poppy" was intended. Others say "poisonous weeds."

With respect to the passage in Amos, some say that "wormwood" as used in the Revised Version was intended. "Wormwood" refers to bitter plants native to desert areas. Belonging to the genus *Artemisia,* they are emblematic of calamity and injustice. The Living Bible refers to the Hebrew translation of "hemlock" as "sour."

Holm Tree

Holm oak, *Quercus ilex,* is one of the finest trees in biblical lands (Josh. 24:26). It had a wide range over the original forests.

This oak is considered as a symbol of sturdiness and strength and was usually planted near solitary tombs.

No mention of this tree is made in the King James Version of the Bible, although the Revised Version includes such in Isaiah 44:14. Some say the oak of Joshua may be a holm tree. The Vulgate renders the name in Isaiah 44:14 as the evergreen oak, *Quercus ilex.*

Judas Tree

Legend has it that Judas hung himself on the Judas tree, *Cercis sp.* This is more fiction than fact. Authorities agree that it was probably not so; yet they do not know what tree was used. Another legend associates his hanging with a fig tree.

Juniper

The juniper of the Bible is not, according to some authorities, the coniferous tree of the genus *Juniperus,* of which several species are native to Lebanon, Galilee, and Basham. Also, juniper is found in semiarid areas and in wilderness wastes.

Scholars say that the plant intended was probably a broom or retama, *Retama roetam.* This is a desert plant with few leaves and would hardly provide respite from the hot sun. In some Bible versions "broom" is used instead of "juniper."

Another view is that it was a juniper, *Juniperus phoenicia,* because of its wilderness association.

In one biblical reference to juniper, Elijah, hunted by
Queen Jezebel and her consort King Ahab of Samaria, went
"a day's journey" into the wilderness. Here he sat down
under a juniper tree and begged the Lord to take his life.
He also laid down and slept under the juniper tree (1 Kings
19:4, 5).

Bewailing his humility, Job said: "Who cut up mallows
by the bushes, and juniper roots for their meat" (Job 30:4).
The outer bark of juniper roots would serve as a temporary
food for one who is hungry.

The juice of the juniper root was used to treat dysentery.
It counteracted the effect of eating tainted meat.

In the Psalms, the statement is made that juniper produces good charcoal fuel (Ps. 120:4). One Bible text says
"with coal of the broom tree."

Laurel

Laurel was the "green bay tree," *Laurus nobilis*. Refer to
the discussion under "bay."

It was the uncommon evergreen much sought after for
perfume, oil, condiments, and medicine. Its leaves and
fruit were used for flavoring pickles.

Laurel is mentioned only once in the Revised Standard
Version of the Bible (Isa. 44:14). In the King James Version
it is referred to as an ash.

Laurel is native to Palestine and other Mediterranean
countries.

Mallow

Mallow, *Atriplex halimus*, is a woody shrub common to
the more salty areas of the holy lands. In the Revised Standard Version of the Bible (Job 30:4), it is referred to as
saltworth.

It is a plant growing in the area referred to by Job. We are
told that hungry shepherds of the desert eat the leaves of
this plant. The leaves are sour and they furnish little
nourishment.

Mastic

Mastic is a fragrant, terebinthine gum which exudes from the pistacia tree. This tree, *Pistacia lentiscus*, grows abundantly in Palestine and Syria. It is mentioned only in the Apocrypha.

Mastic is the universal chewing gum of the East. In early biblical days it was extolled as being good for teeth and gums. A preserve is also made from the gum. Mastic was valued for perfume and for use in medicine.

Meis

Meis is better known in the United States as hackberry, *Celtis sp.*, and to some others in the holy land as "nettle tree."

While this tree is not mentioned in the Bible, there is a question as to whether or not King Solomon considered this tree as sacred. Legend strongly suggests such might be the case.

It is said that Solomon planted two rows of such trees to keep the evil spirits away from the Temple. If this were the case, he could have been influenced by one of his pagan wives.

Presumably several descendants of these trees are still to be found in the vicinity of what was once Solomon's temple area.

Hackberry is one of several "superstitious" trees. In some parts of the biblical area people feel they can sit safely under its branches since no evil spirit will pervade the area. They feel safer while wearing an amulet made from the "sacred" wood.

Mulberry

In King David's battle with the Philistines he inquired of God what to do. God said: "Go not up after them; turn away from them, and come upon them over against the mulberry trees. And it shall be, when thou shalt hear a sound of going in the tops of the mulberry trees, that then thou shalt go out to battle: for God is gone forth before thee to smite the host of the Philistines" (1 Chron. 14: 14, 15).

There is general agreement that the references to mulberry in the King James Version of the Old Testament have no standing (2 Sam. 5:23, 24; I Chron. 14:14, 15). From the Hebrew word "bakha" there is no clue as to what specific tree is meant.

In the Living Bible, however, the reference in 2 Samuel is given as "balsam" while this version maintains the use of "mulberry" in 1 Chronicles.

There is no disagreement that "sycamine" (Luke 17:6) is black mulberry, *Morus nigra*. "Mulberry" is used in the Living Bible. Only one reference is made in the New Testament to "sycamine." Mulberry is mentioned in the Apocrypha (1 Macc. 6:34).

Two major species of mulberry are found in biblical lands. One is the white mulberry, an introduced species, *Morus alba*. Its fruit is pleasant but acid. Black mulberry, a native tree, produces a similar fruit and a much denser shade. For centuries it was, as it is today, especially planted in fig orchards, roofed with vines.

Myrrh

Myrrh is a gum resin extracted from the bark of an Arabian tree, *Balsamodendron myrrh (Fig. 6–19a)*. For centuries the gum was used as a perfume, for embalming, as an incense, and as an ingredient in the holy oil (Exod. 30:23, 25, 34–36; Prov. 7:17; Song of Sol. 3:6; John 19:39). Refer to further comments under "stacte" and "storax."

In biblical times much value was placed on this substance as a commodity. On a monument dedicated to the Egyptian pharaoh Sahure, dating from the twenty-fifth century B.C., there is a record acknowledging the receipt of 80,000 measures of myrrh from the land of Punt, attesting its value in this period.

In 1485 B.C. Queen Hatshepsut obtained and planted thirty-one myrrh trees in front of a steep rock wall west of Thebes, near the temple of Deir-el-Bahri in homage to the god Amon. Until this period they were not grown in Egypt.

Said the psalmist: "All thy garments smell of myrrh and aloes and cassia out of the ivory palaces, whereby they have made thee glad" (Ps. 45:8). Myrrh was esteemed for use in the home, in clothing, on the hair, and in divans and beds. As reported by the adulteress: "I have perfumed my bed with myrrh, aloes, and cinnamon" (Prov. 7:16).

Some botanical authorities indicate that myrrh was obtained from two small, shrubby trees known as *Commiphora myrrha* and *C. erythraea*. They say that the latter named species was the sweet myrrh, and the one of greatest importance in biblical times.

Some say that the myrrh referred to in Genesis 37:25 and 43:11 may be a substance from the tree *Cistus villosus*, a plant growing in abundance in the holy land.

Myrrh is best known as one of the gifts which the wise men presented to Christ at his birth. It was also presented to him, mingled with wine, as he hung on the cross (Mark 15:23), and was one of the ingredients Nicodemus brought to the tomb of Jesus (John 19:39).

Myrtle

Myrtle, *Myrtus communis*, is a well-known small tree of great beauty *(Fig 6-21)*. It is interesting to note that the Hebrew name Esther is derived from this plant. Its Jewish name is "hadassah," meaning the starry white flowers *(Fig. 6-22)*.

Myrtle grows as a shrub or as a tree up to twenty feet in height, and favors a coastal or mountain environment. Its white flowers and aromatic fruits, dried for condiments and perfumes, have always been prized in Bible lands. Though edible, its fruit is astringent.

In his vision, Zechariah saw a rider upon a red horse

Fig. 6–21. Myrtle is a small tree of great beauty. The Hebrew name Esther is derived from this plant. SL

"and he stood among the myrtle trees that were standing in the bottom" (Zech. 1:8).

Myrtle had some religious significance to the Hebrews. It was carried during the Feast of Tabernacles and was used for booths on house tops (Neh. 8:15). To them it typified peace and thanksgiving *(Fig. 6–23).*

In assuring the people of Israel of his protection Jehovah (Yahweh) said: "I will plant in the wilderness the cedar, the shittah tree, and the myrtle, and the oil tree" (Isa. 41:19). Myrtle was also used as an everlasting sign in Isaiah: "and instead of the brier shall come up the myrtle tree."

Myrtle (along with ethrog, palm leaves, and willow branches) was used by the Jews in connection with the tabernacle feast.

Myrtle baths were taken in Syria and Greece for healing purposes.

Oak

Numerous references to oak, *Quercus sp.*, are found throughout the Bible, and this is no doubt due to the extensiveness of the various species in the original mountain forests. Forests of oaks once covered the mountains of Lebanon, Tabor, Gilead, and Carmel as well as the hills of lower Galilee and the area of Hebron. One of the greatest oak forests in ancient times reportedly extended from the Plain of Sharon southerly to the Shagur region. Bozrah was famed for its oaks. It was on the main caravan route across the Syrian Desert, from Damascus to Rabbath-Ammon, and on the route from Nineveh and Babylon. Bozrah was the chief prize of Israel in their conquest of the cities east of the Jordan.

Fig. 6–23. Myrtle branches being sold at a market in Israel. Only choice leaves are acceptable to celebrate the Feast of Tabernacles. To the early Hebrews myrtle signified peace and thanksgiving. CGI

Many species and varieties of oak are native to Palestine and adjacent countries. Among these are *Quercus sessiliflora* found growing on the high Lebanon slopes and in the Hauran, the prickly evergreen oak of Carmel, Bashan, and Gilead, and the deciduous Valonica oak of Galilee and Gilead.

One authority suggests that the oak trees alluded to in the Bible are *Quercus calliprinos (Fig. 6–24)*, the most common oak in Palestine and other Mediterranean countries, and *Q. ithaburensis (Fig. 6–25)*, a tree of low altitudes and less common than the former. However, it is difficult

Fig. 6–24. Acorns and characteristic leaves of Kermes oak, *Quercus calliprinos*, the most common oak in Bible lands. SL

Fig. 6–25. A winter view of Mt. Tabor oak, *Quercus ithaburensis*, in Sharon Park, Israel. It has been suggested that this oak and the Kermes oak, the more prominent oak species in Bible lands, are the oak trees alluded to in the Bible. SL

to distinguish one oak from another in the Bible as it relates to a specific species.

Oak was widely used in biblical times for construction purposes. From the wood carpenters built ships, and oak served as masts and also for oars (Ezek. 27:6, 29). From it charcoal was also produced and extensively employed throughout the region. No doubt the acorns were also used as food by the people.

Some authorities say that the oak of Genesis 35:8 was holly oak, while that of Zechariah 11:2 was the Valonica oak.

Oak has always been characterized as a symbol of strength (Amos 2:9), of long life (Zech. 11:2), and of being graceful (Isa. 61:3). It was also considered a symbol of Israel (Isa. 6:13).

Isaiah placed the oaks of Bashan in the same class as the mighty cedars of Lebanon (2:13), as does Zechariah (11:2).

Jacob buried all the strange gods of his household under an oak which was near Shechem (Gen. 35:4). When Deborah, Rebekah's nurse, died, she was buried near Beth-el under an oak: "and the name of it was called Allon-bachuth" (Gen. 35:8). Allon-bachuth means "oak of weeping."

It has been speculated that Jacob placed the idols under the oak because it was a consecrated tree, and no one would disturb them.

After their defeat by the Philistines, the valiant men of Israel went out on the battlefield to get the desecrated bodies of Saul and his two sons to give them a fitting burial under an oak in Jabesh (1 Chron. 10:12).

When Joshua made a covenant between his people and God he placed a huge rock beneath an oak tree near the sanctuary as a witness to the people (Josh. 24:26).

Abimelech was made king "under the oak of the pillar" (Judg. 9:8) and it was in the branches of an oak tree that the rebellious Prince Absalom, son of David, accidentally hung himself (2 Sam. 18:9).

Perhaps the most famous oaks of the Bible were those associated with Abraham. He "dwelt by the oaks of Mamre which are at Hebron and there built an altar to the LORD" (Gen. 13:18). It was in this tree-clad hill country south of Bethlehem that his son was born. Upon Sarah's death Abraham bought a cave near these oaks which he loved, "the field and the cave that was therein, and all the trees that were in the field" (Gen. 23:17).

Oak groves were also used as places of worship and altars were set up in them (Josh. 24:26).

Oil Tree

There are numerous references in the Bible to the "oil tree"; however, there are questions as to the plant in question. Some think the olive tree was inferred. There is no doubt that Solomon used the wood of the olive tree to make cherubim (1 Kings 6:23), and doors and posts for the Temple (1 Kings 6:31–33).

Some say that oleaster was the "oil tree" to which Isaiah referred (Isa. 41:19). Oleander is not a wild olive but rather a low woody shrub which bears bitter, olive-shaped fruit.

Still others say that the Hebrew word denotes some tree rich in oleaginous or resinous matter, the presence of which is a sign of fertility. This characteristic they assign to the pine, *Pinus halepensis*. The weight of opinion seems to favor this tree as being the "oil tree." It is from this tree that resin and turpentine are obtained.

Today, this pine is widely planted in reforestation programs.

Oleander

There are some who say that the "willows" on which the Hebrews hung their harps were oleanders (Ps. 137:1–3). Majority opinion favors "oleander" as the species.

Oleander, of the family of *Apocynaceae*, is an attractive evergreen. It will grow in sun-baked wadis, providing a refreshing green *(Figs. 6–26* and *6–27).* It is somewhat poisonous.

Bedouins refer to the oleander as "fever flowers." The fever which the people receive is perhaps due to mosquitoes which bite them as they pass by the trees in the evening.

Oleaster

Some believe that the "oil tree" referred to by Isaiah was an oleaster, *Elaeagnus sp.* For comments on this refer to "oil tree."

Olibanum

A small evergreen tree, *Boswellia serrata.* From its bark a resinous gum is obtained. It is believed by some to be the frankincense of the ancients. The gum was chiefly used in incense. See discussion under "frankincense."

Olive

The olive, *Olea europaea (Fig. 6–28),* is the most sacred of all biblical trees. Archeologists say that as early as 4000

Fig. 6–28. Olive trees growing along a road near present-day Beirut. Along with the fig and date palm trees, olive was the most important tree in the biblical period. GG

Fig. 6–26. A wadi, or intermittent stream bed in the Negeb desert of Israel. Pictured is oleander growing in the stream bed. Oleander grows naturally on many of these sites. It is thought by some that this plant, rather than willow, is the one upon which the Hebrews hung their harps as they sat down and wept for their homeland. GGI

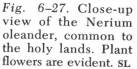

Fig. 6–27. Close-up view of the Nerium oleander, common to the holy lands. Plant flowers are evident. SL

B.C. the olive was in large scale production in the lower Euphrates region. Olive kernels have been found in excavations of Meggido, a city dating back to 3200 B.C.

It has been a companion of man through the centuries. Its habitat is the hilly Mediterranean area from Spain to Samaria, Italy, and Greece. Rarely is it found growing under natural conditions beyond 2000 feet in elevation. It is a coastal species, in that mists from the sea are essential to its natural growth and survival.

The olive was universally cultivated in Bible lands (Rom. 11:24).

The tree has a gnarled, unshapely form and a coarse bark, with silver green leaves. It is a long-lived species. Some olive trees reach the age of 1000 or more years. Before a mature tree dies, it usually sends up new shoots *(Figs. 6–29 and 6–30)*. Wood from the tree is knotty and brittle.

Fig. 6–29. Suckering from a young olive tree. Suckering is a characteristic of the olive. CGI

Fig. 6–30 Before the mature olive tree dies it usually sends up new shoots to continue its life. These olive trees are near Karmiel, in the area of Galilee.

בָּנֶיךָ כִּשְׁתִלֵי זֵיתִים
סָבִיב לְשֻׁלְחָנֶךָ
תהילים/קכ"ח ג

THY CHILDREN LIKE OLIVE PLANTS
ROUND ABOUT THY TABLE
PSALMS 128:3

The fruit, or olive berry, is a drupe that is black when fully ripe. It matures in November.

The chief value of the tree is the oil pressed from its fruit. It is the chief article of commerce wherever olive trees are grown. Large groves exist today in the vicinity of most Mediterranean cities, along the coasts of Syria and Palestine, and throughout the hilly terrain of Lebanon. For generations olives have yielded oil for lamps in homes and the Temple (Lev. 24:2).

Olive oil makes up a large part of the diet of the people in Bible lands. It is used in salads, for frying, and as a butter substitute. A large amount of the oil today is also used in the manufacture of soap. Olives are used widely as a food as well. They are eaten after pickling in brine, or in a ripe condition when preserved in olive oil. In its excellent pottery ancient Greece shipped olive oil all over that part of the world with which she had commerce. The oil was also used in bathing feet (Deut. 33:24).

Shepherds today still carry such simple foods as olives, bread, cheese, and dried figs.

Disaster to a crop of olives was a cause of ruin and considered a sign of divine wrath.

The olive is often alluded to in the Bible as an emblem of prosperity and wealth, and much is said as to its beauty, fruitfulness, and usefulness to man (Ps. 128:3; Jer. 11:16; Hos. 14:6). It was also a symbol of divine blessing (Judg. 9:8, 9) and of peace (Gen. 8:11; Neh. 8:15).

The dove brought back an olive leaf to the ark which proved to Noah that "the waters were abated from off the earth" (Gen. 8:11). Olive branches were used in making booths "for the feast of the seventh month" (Neh. 8:14, 15).

In King Solomon's Temple olive wood was used for making the cherubim, doors, and posts (1 Kings 6:23; 31–35). Solomon's payment to Hiram was, in part, pure beaten olive oil, paid year by year, for twenty years.

In Christ's time newly born babies were bathed and rubbed with olive oil and salt (Ezek. 16:4). It was said this

Fig. 6–31. Church of All Nations in Jerusalem. Mount of Olives in background. GG

hardened the muscles. Following this, they were wrapped in swaddling clothes.

Perhaps the best-known olive trees were those which grew on the Mount of Olives *(Fig. 6–31).* It was after the institution of the Lord's Supper, "when they had sung a hymn," that Jesus led his disciples "over the brook Cedron ... out into the Mount of Olives ... to a garden called Gethsemane" (John 18:1; Matt. 26:30, 36).

The Mount of Olives, called Olivet, was associated with Jesus in other remarkable events: his triumphal entry into Jerusalem (Matt. 21:1; Mark 11:1; Luke 10:29), the prediction of Jerusalem's overthrow (Mark 13:1), and his ascension (Acts 1:11, 12).

In ancient times a stranger entering a city or town usually carried an olive branch in his hand in the sacred character of a supplicant. This practice assured him of greater safety than if he entered without such.

The well-known Hippocrates and his brother, in the year

500, opened the gates of Herbessus and came forward as supplicants to the invading Syracusan army. In their hands they held branches of olive, tufted with wool, an apparent well-known sign of a supplicant during this period.

Opobalsamum

See discussion under "Balm of Gilead" and "Stacte."

Palm

Refer to discussion under "date palm." The palm will grow to a height of 100 feet, with leaves up to 6 feet in length. It has no branches.

Pine

While several species of pine are native to the holy lands, there seems to be dispute among authorities as to the reference to pine in Nehemiah 8:15 and Isaiah 41:19. Some say that in the original Hebrew, neither passage signifies pine. Another says that the reference in Nehemiah is to "fat wood," or a pine. Still another says the Isaiah reference refers to a plane tree.

There is general agreement that the reference to pine for use in beautifying the Sanctuary is correct (Isa. 60:13). It is thought to have been Aleppo pine, *Pinus halepensis* (*Fig. 6–32*). Yet, one authority believes it might be a fir. Some authorities consider pine as an "oil tree."

Recent archeological studies of sunken vessels in the Mediterranean Sea show that Aleppo pine was extensively used in making the hulls of merchant ships in the period 2000 B.C.

Pistacia (Pistachio)

The pistacia tree grew in ancient Bible lands and pistacia nuts were among the gifts which Jacob sent to Joseph in Egypt (Gen. 43:11). It is sometimes referred to as pistachio or pistache.

Pistacia is a small tree. The nuts, or seeds, contain two

Fig. 6–32. An old, veteran Aleppo pine located near
the Rockefeller Museum in Tel Aviv, Israel. It is one
of the oldest living specimens in this nation. During
the early biblical period it was a common species in
the high mountains. SL

cotyledons. The nuts are salted in brine while still in the shell and are prized for their resinous flavor.

There are several species of pistacia. Majority opinion is that the pistacia of the Bible was *Pistacia vera*. Some say, however, that the species *P. palaestina (Fig. 6–33)* or *P. atlantica* may have been intended. However, the latter have fruit that is less tasty and smaller than *P. vera*.

One pistacia species, *Pistacia texana,* is native to the United States. It is found only in Texas.

Plane

The plane tree, *Platanus orientalis,* grown as an ornamental in the United States, is indigenous to the holy lands. It is primarily a water-loving species and is found principally along the banks of streams. It grows in Palestine and other parts of the Bible lands where soil conditions will permit.

While the plane tree is not specifically mentioned in the Bible, most authorities agree that the references to chestnut in Genesis (30:37) and Ezekiel (31:8) are mistranslations of the original Hebrew. They hold to the view that the plane tree was intended. Refer to discussion under "chestnut."

In the Genesis account, Jacob used branches of the tree as part of his scheme to trick Laban in Haran. Ezekiel likens Pharaoh to the plane and other trees in the garden of God.

The plane tree was well-known to the Romans. In the days of Pliny they were planted around schools in Athens. Herodotus says that·when Xerxes invaded Greece he was so enchanted by a particular plane tree that he encircled it with a collar of gold and confided the charge of it to one of his ten thousand.

Pomegranate

While the pomegranate, *Punica granatum (Fig. 6–34),* is not a favorite fruit in the United States, trees are widely

Fig. 6–33. A young, vigorous growing pistacia tree,
Pistacia palaestina. SL

Fig. 6–34. Fruit of the pomegranate tree. USDA

cultivated and their fruit consumed in Bible lands. It has a long history of use. The tree was grown in the Hanging Gardens of Babylon.

Grown widely as an ornamental, the pomegranate tree has bright green leaves and a reddish decorative fruit. The fruit has a woody astringent covering enclosing a large number of pulpy seeds of a pinkish color.

The fruit was used for the making of wine and it had medical properties. The rind contains a high content of tannin and from it a concoction was prepared for use as a remedy against the tapeworm.

There are numerous references to "pomegranate" in the Bible. It was among the fruits the spies brought back to Moses from the land of Canaan (Num. 13:20). Saul tarried under a pomegranate tree while in battle with the Philistines (1 Sam. 14:2). Aaron wore a priestly garment, the hem of which was adorned with woven pomegranate fruit designs (Exod. 28:33, 34). King Solomon also adorned the Temple with reliefs *(Fig. 6–35)* of 200 pomegranates (1 Kings 7:18, 20) and called the fruit of the tree the most pleasant (Song of Sol. 4:13).

In art, the pomegranate is a symbol of health and longevity. In mythology, it was used as a symbol of fertility.

According to an early Jewish ordinance, the paschal lamb was roasted on a spit of pomegranate wood, the spit passing through the mouth to the vent.

In early biblical times the pomegranate was considered by some as the Tree of Life.

Poplar

While poplar grows on moist sites in Bible lands, there is a question among authorities as to the species alluded to in Genesis 30:37 and Hosea 4:13. See comments under "chestnut."

Some believe that the storax tree, *Styrax officinalis,* was intended. Although generally a shrub, it can grow to a height of twenty feet. The lower surface of the leaves is

Fig. 6–35. The pomegranate fruit was widely used by the Jews in reliefs on important structures. This view is of a relief from an ancient synagogue unearthed at Capernaum. It is said that Christ may have preached in the old structure. Pomegranates, grapes, palm, and figs will be noted in the relief.

whitish and the tree bears a large number of white flowers. This, they say, could be a "white tree," being a close translation of the Hebrew word in the scriptural passages.

Others say it is the white poplar, *Populus alba,* common along the streams in Bible lands. It has a whitish inner bark, and the wood would be of white color when the bark is peeled away. Weight of authority is with the poplar. However, since *P. euphratica* is the only species of poplar indigenous to Israel, this is the most likely species.

It was the branches of poplar trees, along with those from the almond and plane trees, that were used by Jacob in Haran in his scheme to increase his flocks more than Laban's (Gen. 30:37)

In more ancient periods poplar was used extensively in building construction.

Shittim

Shittim is one of the names given to the wood which comes from the acacia tree, *Acacia raddiana.* Two other species, *A. seyal,* and *A. tortilis,* are native to the deserts of Sinai and around the Dead Sea. Refer to discussion under "acacia."

Shittim is mentioned twenty-six times in the Bible in connection with the tabernacle and its furnishings.

Acacia wood is hard, heavy, close-ringed, and insect resistant. When first cut it is yellowish-brown in color but with age turns blackish. The grain of the wood made it most suitable for the construction of the tabernacle and furnishings. The wood was also used for tanning leather, for fuel, and for parts of mummy cases.

Also known as the shitta tree, shittam tree, and shittah tree, acacia occurs and grows well in dry arid areas and reaches heights of up to twenty feet. The flowers of such trees are yellow. It produces a gum arabic.

Like some other biblical trees, habitations or places were named from this tree. Shittam, Abel-Shittim, and the

Valley of Shittim were so named. Abel-Shittim means a "meadow of acacia." This location was the last stop of the people of Israel in the wilderness, prior to crossing the Jordan into the Promised Land (Num. 25:1; 33:49).

Moses solicited from the Hebrew people shittim wood, as an offering for use in construction of the tabernacle (Exod. 25:5). The Ark was made of it (see *Fig. 6–36*), as well as other furnishings (Exod. 25:10, 23; 26:15, 26; 38:1).

"I will plant in the wilderness the cedar, the shittah tree, and the myrtle, and the oil tree," said Jehovah (Yahweh) in giving Israel his protection (Isa. 41:18).

Within the Ark of the Covenant were placed Aaron's rod, the "golden pot that contained manna," the holy anointing oil, and the tables of stone. Yet when King Solomon

Fig. 6–36. The Ark of the Covenant was made from acacia, or shittim wood, as it is sometimes called. This carving of the Ark is located at Capernaum and is numbered among many other Jewish symbols found at this site.

brought the Ark into the Temple only the two tables of stone were found in it (1 Kings 8:9). The Bible is silent as to what disposition was made of the other items.

It is a tradition of the Jews that the Ark was hidden by Josiah when Jerusalem was taken by the Chaldeans and will be restored in the days of the Messiah.

Stacte

Stacte was one of the four aromatic ingredients used in the holy oil in the Tabernacle of the Congregation (Exod. 30:34–36). The Revised Version of the Bible refers to it as being "opobalsamum." However, there is general agreement among authorities that it was not this, nor was it storax from the plant called *Styrax benzion*.

Josephus said opobalsamum grew in the city of Engedi, 300 furlongs from Jerusalem. Said he: "In that place grows the best kind of palm trees and the opobalsamum."

According to some authorities, stacte is the myrrh of the Bible. Myrrh was one of the gifts presented to Christ at his birth by the wise men *(Fig. 6–19a)*. Refer to "myrrh."

Storax

The storax tree, *Styrax officinalis,* is a shrub or small tree common to biblical lands. It is thought by some that the "poplar" of Genesis 30:37 and Hosea 4:13 was storax. However, the weight of authority is against this.

Storax did produce a gum used in perfumes.

There is general agreement that storax did not produce the "stacte" of the Old Testament incense (Exod. 30:34). Refer to the discussion under "stacte."

Sycamine

Sycamine is mentioned but once in the Bible, and that in the New Testament. Said the Lord with reference to this tree: "If ye had faith as a grain of mustard seed, ye might say unto this sycamine tree, Be thou plucked up by the root, and be thou planted in the sea; and it should obey you" (Luke 17:6).

In this case the Lord had reference to black mulberry, *Morus nigra*, according to biblical authorities. Black mulberry is abundant in Palestine. Refer to comments under "mulberry."

Sycamore

The sycamore mentioned in the Bible is not the sycamore as known in our country, *Platanus sp.* Rather, the term sycamore or its common name "sycomore," are synonymous and refer to a fig tree which formerly grew extensively in Bible lands, *Ficus sycomorus (Fig. 6–37).* Its

Fig. 6–37. The sycamore tree, a fig, that once grew abundantly in Bible lands. This tree, located in Tel Aviv, is currently protected by the government of Israel. Few trees of this size have survived.

habitat is the lowlands and coastal plains where the trees escape frost (Ps. 78:47). It is a spreading tree and widely planted along roadsides. The wood of the tree is light and was used to some extent in carpentry. It was also used for fuel.

Sycamore was once abundant in the holy lands (1 Kings 10:27; 2 Chron. 1:15; 9:27) and in Egypt (Ps. 78:47). The trees are subject to killing by heavy frosts (Ps. 78:47).

Zaccheus brought fame to the sycamore, for it was he who climbed into its branches that he might better see Jesus as the Lord passed that way (Luke 19:4).

Amos was a "gatherer of sycamore fruit" (Amos 8:14), attesting the edibility of the fruit. That sycamore was an important food crop is shown by King David's appointment of an overseer for the trees in the Shephelah (1 Chron. 27:28; Ps. 78:47; Isa. 9:10).

Sycamore is inferior to the common fig.

Sycomore

Sycomore is a species of fig, *Ficus sycomorus*, indigenous to Bible lands. The word "sycomore" is a name commonly applied to the "sycamore" of the Bible and is reflected in its scientific name. It is not related to the sycamore, *Platanus sp.*, with which we are familiar in the United States. In the sycomore, or sycamore, figs are found in dense clusters on older branches and are much smaller and inferior in taste and sugar content than those of the better known fig, *Ficus carica*. Notwithstanding, they are widely eaten.

Sycomore wood is extremely durable. Mummy coffins made of this wood have been found in old Egyptian tombs. The wood also has been used in making furniture and for general construction purposes.

Sycomore is said to be native to tropical Africa.

Refer to comments under "sycamore" and to the chapter on the "Dresser of the Sycamore."

Fig. 6–38. A tamarisk tree, *Tamarix aphylla*, common to Israel.

Tamarisk

The tamarisk tree, *Tamarix aphylla (Fig. 6–38),* is not referred to in the King James Version of the Bible. However, there is general agreement among biblical authorities that a correct rendering of the Hebrew makes it applicable to Genesis 21:33, 1 Samuel 22:6 and 31:3 and Jeremiah 48:6.

A number of species of tamarisk are found in biblical

lands. Several occur in Palestine alone. *Tamarix manni-fera,* common to the Sinai Desert, is said by some authorities to be the one that produced the "manna" of the Exodus. *T. pentandra, T. pallasii,* and *T. aphylla* are three other common species.

Tamarisk is small of stature, a bushy plant with pink and white flowers. Arabs consider this tree holy since in the spring, when the wind blows, it branches are thought to say "Allah."

It was at Beer-sheba that Abraham planted a tamarisk tree and called there on the name of the Lord, the everlasting God (Gen. 21:33). Abraham may have attached some religious significance to this tree.

Under a tamarisk tree at Jabesh were placed the bones of Saul and his sons. Following the burial the group fasted, in accordance with their ritual, for seven days (1 Sam. 31:13).

Saul, in pursuit of David to kill him, rested in an "abode in Gibeah under a tamarisk tree in Ramah" (1 Sam. 23:6), and his bones were buried beneath another tree in Jabesh-gilead (1 Sam. 31:13). In the King James Version this is referred to as a "tree."

That tamarisk was common to the desert is shown by Jeremiah 17:6. It grows abundantly in deserts, on sand dunes, in salt marshes, and along rivers. Tamarisk was extensively used for building construction.

Several species of tamarisk or tamarix, as it is sometimes called, are grown in the U.S. for ornamental purposes. They grow readily from cuttings. The common salt-cedar of the Southwest, *Tamarix pentandra,* has become naturalized over an extensive area.

Tamarix

Refer to discussion under "tamarisk."

Teil

With reference to the teil tree, Isaiah said: "—as a teil tree, and as an oak, whose substance is in them, when they cast their leaves; so the holy seed shall be the substance thereof" (Isa. 6:13).

There is general agreement among authorities that the Hebrew interpretation of the word in the passage would more aptly apply to the terebinth tree. The oaklike terebinth yields a resinous substance which has given it a local name of "turpentine tree." Yet others say an oak may have been implied.

There are those who believe it was a terebinth tree, not an oak, under which Jacob hid the strange gods and earrings of his idolatrous household near Shechem (Gen. 35:4).

Other authorities say that "teil" is an obsolete name for the lime or linden tree, *Tilia europea.*

Terebinth

Only in the Apocrypha (Eccls. 24:16) is mention made of the terebinth tree, a pistacia. *Pistacia terebinthus,* and *P. mutica,* are two common species. The latter is more common east of the Jordan and in Jebel Bilas of the Syrian desert. Other pistacia species indigenous to Bible lands are *P. vera, P. palaestina,* and *P. atlantica.* Refer to comments under "pistacia."

Some authorities hold the opinion that several oak references in the Bible may properly refer to this tree (Isa. 6:13; Hos. 4:13). It is so rendered in the Revised Version by marginal notations.

Josephus reported on what is considered a terebinth tree near Hebron. Said he: "There is, at a distance of six furlongs from the city, a very large turpentine tree; some of the ancients call this famous tree, or grove, an oak; others, a turpentine tree, or grove. It has been very famous in all past ages, and is so, I suppose, at this day, and that particularly for an eminent mart or meeting of merchants there every year, as the travellers inform us. And the report goes, that this tree has continued ever since the creation of the world."

One biblical authority says the Valley of Elah (1 Sam. 17:2, 19; 21:9) probably refers to a valley noted for its "terebinths," though none are there today.

Fruit of the pistacia is globular and stony. These trees have an acrid odor somewhat like turpentine. Such would be similar to the native Texas species.

Thick Tree

There appears to be no identification of the "thick trees" referred to in the Bible (Lev. 23:40; Neh. 8:15). The Revised Standard Version refers to such as "leafy trees."

As reported in Leviticus: "And ye shall take you on the first day the boughs of goodly trees, branches of palm trees, and the boughs of thick trees, and willows of the brook; and ye shall rejoice before the Lord your God seven days" (23:40).

One authority suggests that the reference might refer to myrtle, but this is probably not the case since, in Nehemiah, "myrtle" and "thick trees" are listed separately.

Thorny Shrubs

These are not an individual species, but rather many. They are included in this listing because of the many biblical references to them (Fig. 6–39). Such woody shrubs are widespread throughout Bible lands. Cattle and goats use some of them as food.

Thorny shrubs and briers were suggested by Gideon as being suitable threshing instruments to torture the flesh of his enemies (Judg. 8:7). Thorns were likely what women used under their cook-pots.

The shrubs did provide a hot, quick fire for outdoor ovens in biblical lands (Ps. 58:9; Nah. 1:10). King David referred to them as being difficult to touch (2 Sam. 23:7).

Thorns on the altars of Israel were evidences of sin. Micah spoke of wicked men as worse than a thorny hedge (Micah 7:4). Isaiah refers to thorns as a symbol of utter destruction (Isa. 24:13).

Thorny hedges were used around gardens (Hos. 2:6).

The thorns of Isaiah 34:13 and Hosea 2:6, among others, are thought to be the woody shrub *Poterium spinosum*. A plant about two feet in height, it has many thorns. It is common to Palestine and used as fuel and for fencing.

A recent Jewish writer relates, by simile, a thorny plant, Gagal, to that of "rolling thing" in Isaiah 17:13. Said Isaiah: "The nations shall rush like the rushing of many waters: but God shall rebuke them, and they shall flee far off, and shall be chased as the chaff of the mountains before the

Fig. 6–39. Many thorny shrubs of various species adorn the landscape of deserts. Pictured are some of the thorny plants in the Negev desert. They are more abundant on the site shown due to the presence of ground moisture. The palm tree pictured here reflects the presence of moisture. Many references to thorny plants and their uses are found in the Bible. SGI

wind, and like a rolling thing before the whirlwind" *(Fig. 6–40).*

The gagal is a small, menacing looking, thorny plant found on the more arid sites in Israel. In late summer it dries up but appears firmly entrenched in the soil. However, an abscissa layer of cells forms between the main stem and the roots. When this happens, a strong late summer wind will cause the top of the plant to blow away.

As interpreted by the Jewish writer: "So it will be with Israel's enemies. They look very menacing but they have no real roots in the land, and so shall they be swept away like the gagal before the wind. And it shall happen quickly. At evening, lo, terror! By morning it is no more."

Thyine

Thyine is a much prized, highly aromatic wood obtained from a large tree known as *Collistris quadrivalvis.* It was marketed as an article of commerce in mystic Babylon (Rev. 18:12) and was widely traded by Rome. Today it is known as sandarac due to the resin it produces. This resin is used in making varnish. It is also used as an incense.

Imported from Africa, the wood was prized by Romans as an expensive luxury. It was used by them in the manufacture of furniture, particularly tables. Because of its scent, the wood was also utilized by the Greeks in connection with temple worship.

The wood is reddish brown, hard, and has a wavy grain. It takes a hard polish.

The Revised Standard Version refers to thyine as "scented wood."

Turpentine Tree

This tree is referred to only in the Apocrypha (Eccls. 24:16). It is said to be the terebinth, *Pistacia terebinthus,* and its variety *P. palestina.*

It is a tree that grows solitary from other trees, not in pure stands.

Fig. 6–40. Gagal or rolling plant, *Salsola kali,* of Israel. They roll in the wind as do the so-called "tumble weeds" of the American Southwest. Isaiah refers to the gagal as the chaff of the mountains. Bottom photo shows relative size of plant. SL

Another species, *P. mutica,* is reportedly more common east of the Jordan and in the Jebel Bilas of the Syrian Desert.

Certain authorities say that some of the words translated "oak" in the Authorized Version of the Bible may be better translated "pistacia."

An interesting but doubtful report on a turpentine tree is reported by Josephus. He said: "There is also showed, at the distance of six furlongs from the city, a very large turpentine tree; and the report goes, that this tree has continued ever since the creation of the world."

See discussion under "terebinth."

Walnut

Walnut, *Juglans regia,* is a tree prized for its nuts. Walnuts grew along the shores of Galilee and probably in Solomon's garden (Isa. 6:11). The nuts are very nutritious and contain a high percentage of fat. Josephus reports they were widely cultivated in his time.

From the husks of the walnut seed a brownish dye was obtained. It was used for dyeing homespun, seamless cloaks. One writer has suggested that Christ's garments may have been dyed brown.

It was common practice to beat the nuts from the tree with sticks rather than picking them up from the ground when they fell naturally. The belief was that this practice made the tree grow better.

Weeping Willow

Contrary to a widely held belief, the weeping willow, *Salix babylonica (Fig. 6–42),* did not grow in ancient Bible lands. It is a native of China.

Some have said that it was the weeping willow trees upon which the Hebrews hung their harps (Ps. 137: 1, 2), but such could not be the case.

Fig. 6-41. One of the most common willows in the holy lands. Willow played an important role in the religious festivals of the early Hebrews. SL

Willow

Many species of the willow tree grow throughout the world and the Bible lands are no exception. Several are common along the Jordan River. *Salix acmophylla (Fig. 6–41)* reaches a height of about seventy-five feet and is the most common.

Willow played an important role in the religious festivals of the early Hebrews. "Willows of the brook," in the Hebrew ritual of worship, were waved for joy. In the right hand every worshiper carried a "lulab" during the Feast of Tabernacles (Lev. 23:40). The "lulab" was composed of palm, with myrtle and a willow branch on either side of the palm. It was shaken at an appropriate place in the ceremony. The "lulab" was used in the temple on each of the seven festive days.

Job refers to the protective covering afforded by willows when he said: "The shady trees cover him with their shadow; the willows of the brook compass him about" (Job 40:22). One writer has suggested that the "willows" reference in this passage might well be a "poplar," *Populus euphratica,* since it was common on the shores of the "waters of Babylon." However, majority opinion favors "willow."

Isaiah prophesied the coming prosperity of Israel in terms of willows when he said: "And they shall spring up as among the grass, as willows by the water courses" (Isa. 44:4).

Ezekiel's parable of the willows is related to his dream of abundant water and productive soil (Ezek. 17:5).

It is evident that the willow was a popular tree since many places in the Scriptures were named from willow.

Excavation of the tomb of the Sumerian Queen Shub-ad who lived in the period 5000 B.C. revealed a crown on which were engraved willow leaves. Other crowns had beech leaves similarly engraved.

Fig. 6–42. This is a weeping willow growing in the city of Jerusalem. It was not a part of the original vegetation of the Bible lands during early Hebrew days. Therefore, it could not be the tree upon which the Hebrews hung their harps. SL

Wormwood

Bitter plants growing in waste, usually desert places, are referred to as wormwood. They belong to the genus *Artemisia* of which there are reportedly five principal species in the tablelands and deserts of Palestine and Syria. *Artemisia herba-alba*, a common species, is an aromatic shrub. It has a bitter taste and is used in folk medicine. *A. Monosperma (Fig. 6–43)* is another common species.

Wormwood, as a bitter plant, was considered by the Hebrews to be an emblem of calamity and injustice.

Throughout the Bible bitterness is symbolic of affliction,

misery, servitude (Exod. 1:14; Ruth 1:20; Prov. 5:4), wickedness (Jer. 4:18), and a time of mourning and lamentation (Amos 8:10).

It was because of the symbolic meaning of bitterness that bitter herbs were commanded to be used in the celebration of the Passover (Exod. 12:8; Num. 9:11). The ordinance was to remind the Hebrews of their bitter bondage (Exod. 1:14) and of the haste with which they made their escape from Egypt.

The extent to which the Hebrews used wormwood in any celebration is unknown. Obviously, they were well aware of its bitterness. Such plants as watercress, endive, and pepper grass, among others, are known to have been used as "bitter plants" during the Passover.

Specific references to wormwood in the Scriptures mention it as a symbol of evil (Deut. 29:18); a symbol of punishment and suffering (Jer. 9:15; 23:15); denoting offensiveness (Amos 5:7); the fate of a sinful woman (Prov. 5:4); and affliction (Lam. 3:15, 19). In Revelation (8:11), a star is called Wormwood. This passage also refers to waters that became wormwood and in which men died because they were made bitter.

A European species of wormwood, A. *absinthium*, is a commercial source of medical oils and Absinthe, an intoxicating liquor. An American range species, A. *frigida*, called fringed wormwood, was used by Indians and early American settlers to make decoctions for the treatment of colds, as a diuretic and mild cathartic.

Of interest is that the genus name of wormwood is derived from Artemisia, wife of King Mausolus. Our word "mausoleum" was first used with reference to the tomb of King Mausolus and his wife of Caria in Asia Minor. It was erected at Halicarnassus in 353 B.C. The tomb, or monument, was considered as one of the seven wonders of the world.

A species of wormwood, A. *abrotanum*, (*Fig. 6–44*) has

Fig. 6–43. Wormwood in the desert of the Sinai. No doubt Moses was familiar with this plant during his stay in the wilderness. SL

been introduced into the United States for erosion control of road cut banks in arid areas. It is also used as an ornamental.

An extraction of wormwood is an essential ingredient of vermouth.

Fig. 6–44. Wormwood is a bitter woody plant that grows in desert places. It was considered by the Hebrews as an emblem of calamity and injustice. The species pictured here is known as Big Sage, *Artemisia tridentata,* closely resembling the wormwood with which Moses and the prophets were familiar.

7

🍁 Tree
Gardens

CONTRARY TO THE ACCEPTED DEFINITION OF "garden" today, records of the past show that the gardens of the oldest civilizations were made up of trees and scented shrubs (Eccl. 2:5; Song of Sol. 4:13; Neh. 2:8). Shade, scent, and water were the primary requisites in old Eastern gardens. Yet, flowers, herbs, and vegetables were also cultivated in some areas nearby, or in conjunction with them (Song of Sol. 5:1; 6:2).

Tree gardens most generally adjoined the residences of the wealthy or influential persons. The kings' gardens were elaborate, much like a private park (2 Kings 25:14). They were usually watered by irrigation (Isa. 58:11). Egyptian gardens were highly dependent upon a water source. Such gardens in Egypt were dedicated to the god Khem. He was the deity of gardens.

Frequently the garden was fenced with a stone or mud

159

wall (Prov. 24:31) or thorny hedges (Isa. 5:5) and protected by a watchman in a tower (Mark 12:1) or lodge (Isa. 1:8). One of the duties of the watchman was to drive away wild beasts and robbers. Our word "garden" derives from the word "guarded."

Historical reports reveal that scarecrows were used to keep birds away from fruit plants in a garden.

To one who could afford it, a tree garden permitted him to walk in the shade and be much cooler. It was an outdoor area where one could have social events. Where water was available for irrigation, a pool would be built and serve as a place for bathing.

Fruit, olive and nut trees, and scented shrubs were principally planted in gardens. Grapes were often planted. After they were grown, a wine press often became part of the garden. Yet, there were instances, as reported elsewhere in this book, where trees were planted for wood production.

Date palms, of high importance for food, were garden trees. Additionally, the trunk could be used for beams in construction, branches to serve as roofing material, and leaves for brooms and baskets. Second in importance was the sycamore fig and pomegranate.

The luxury garden of Amun, in the old city of Pi-Raamses, in the delta of Egypt, employed 8000 slaves in its care and maintenance. Use of slave labor for this purpose was common among the conquerors.

Epicurus (342–271 B.C.), a philosopher in Athens, had a garden in which he expounded his materialistic views. It is said his garden rivaled in popularity the Academy of his time. His followers, called Epicureans, were addressed by Paul (Acts. 17:18).

Gardens were also used for worship and as burial places (2 Kings 21:18; John 19:41—see *Fig. 7–1*). The field of Machpelah, Abraham's burial ground, was a natural garden, with trees in and around it (Gen. 23:17). Manasseh

Fig. 7–1. "Now in the place where he was crucified there was a garden; and in the garden a new sepulchre, wherein was never man yet laid" (John 19:41). Pictured is the garden as it appears today, in the area where Christ was presumably entombed.

and Amon were buried in Uzza's garden (2 Kings 21:18, 26).

Jesus often went to the Garden of Gethsemane for meditation and prayer. As recorded by Mark, "He went forth with his disciples over the brook Cedron, where was a garden, into which he entered, and his disciples. And Judas also, which betrayed him, knew the place: for Jesus ofttimes resorted thither with his disciples" (John 18:1, 2).

Several symbolic references are made to gardens in the Bible. In one the believer is likened to a garden watered by the Holy Spirit (Jer. 2:13; 17:7, 8; John 4:13, 14). Another passage states that a well-watered garden expresses happiness and prosperity (Isa. 58:11; Jer. 31:12) in contrast to a garden with no water which expresses spiritual, national, and individual barrenness and misery (Isa. 1:30).

A twelfth century writer had this to say: "A noble garden will give you medlars, quinces, the pearmain, peaches, pears of St. Regle, pomegranates, citrons, oranges, almonds, dates, and figs." Apparently the affluent in this period of history held to the same concept of a garden as those in the biblical period.

It may aptly be stated that the human race had its origin in a garden of trees. Christ suffered in a garden. He was crucified in one. Lastly, it was in a garden that he was buried. And, we assume paradise to be a garden.

Christ and the Garden of Mataria

Although we have no historical proof, there is a legend of long standing to the effect that Christ, when a babe, spent his time in the herbal gardens of Mataria in Egypt. Mataria is a village about 2000 years old, about six miles north of the present-day city of Cairo *(Fig. 7–2)*.

Says the biblical narration: "And when they were departed, behold, the angel of the Lord appeared to Joseph in a dream, saying, Arise, and take the young child and his mother, and flee into Egypt, and be thou there until I bring thee word: for Herod will seek the young child to destroy him. When he arose, he took the young child and his mother by night and departed into Egypt" (Matt. 2:13, 14).

Where Joseph and his family stayed in Egypt is speculation. The Bible does not say, neither is there any other historical record on the subject. Yet it would be obvious that they would prefer to stay in an area occupied by people of their own nationality. Such an area could have been the herbal gardens of Mataria on the east bank of the Nile River.

Josephus stated that Cleopatra took cuttings of balsam bushes from Jericho to Egypt. These were planted in the

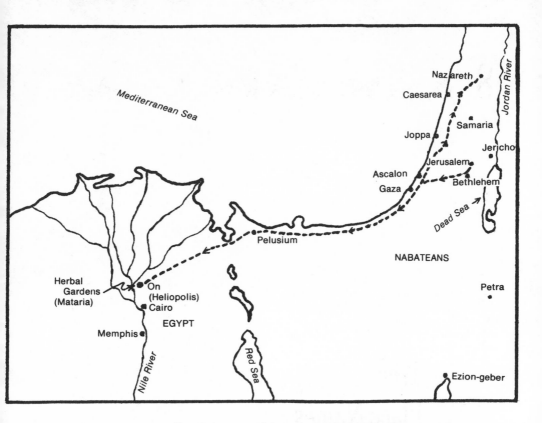

Fig. 7–2. According to legend, Joseph, Mary, and the baby Jesus resided in the herbal gardens of Mataria during their sojourn in Egypt. Indicated on the map is a possible route from Bethlehem to Egypt and return to Nazareth. Joseph chose to return to Nazareth since this town was under the milder rule of Herod Antipas. Trees and other woody plants were grown in the herbal garden.

temple gardens at Heliopolis. This is the "On" of the Bible (Gen. 41:50). They were planted and cared for by the skilled Jewish gardeners from the Jordan valley. The rare and precious shrubs thrived along the Nile under the care given them.

It was about thirty years later, according to the legend, when Joseph, Mary, and Jesus found refuge in this garden during their sojourn in Egypt.

Perhaps we may never know if this legend of the Mataria garden is true.

8

 Tree
Place Names

WITHIN THE PAGES OF THE BIBLE there are a number of Hebrew place names related to trees, or compounded with such names *(Fig. 8–1)*. Among these are:

Abel Shittim. *Meadow of acacia.* The last stopping place of Israel (Num. 33:49)

Atad. *A thorn.* Said to be a descriptive appellation given to a thorny location (Gen. 50:10, 11)

Baal-tamar. *Lord of the palm trees.* One of the groves of palm trees northeast of Jerusalem on the ruined site of Erhah.

Baca. *Balsam tree.* The Baca Valley of Palestine (Ps. 84:6)

Beth shittah. *House of acacia.* Point to which the Midianites fled from Gideon (Judg. 7:22)

Beth tappuah. *House of apples.* A town west of Hebron (Josh. 15:53)

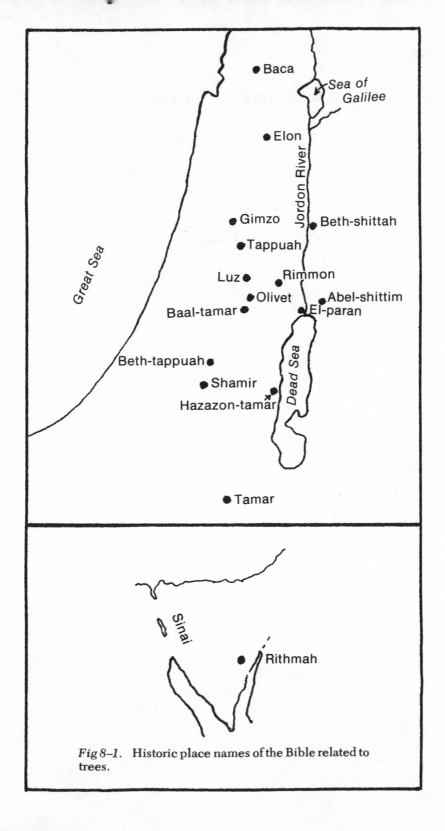

Fig 8–1. Historic place names of the Bible related to trees.

Elah. *Oak* or large evergreen (terebinth). Vale of Elah (1 Sam. 17:2; 21:9)

Elath. *Great trees.* Same as Eloth. Town of Elath (1 Kings 9:26)

Elim. *Trees.* Where the Israelites encamped for a month in the desert. (Exod. 15:27; Num. 33:9; Exod. 16:1)

Elon. *Oak.* A town on the boundary of the tribe of Dan (Josh. 19:43)

Eloth. *Great trees.* Another form of Elath (1 Kings 9:26)

En-tappuah. *Abundance of apples.* Located near Tappuah (Josh. 17:7)

El-paran. *Oak of Paran.* An oasis in the wilderness (Gen. 14:5, 6)

En-rimmon. *Fountain of a pomegranate.* Place occupied by descendants of Judah after the exile (Neh. 11:29)

Gath-rimmon. *Press of pomegranate.* A Levitical city of the tribe of Dan (Josh. 19:45; 21:24; 1 Chron. 6:69)

Gimzo. *A place abounding in sycamores.* A town in the low country of Judah (2 Chron. 28:18)

Hazazon-tamar. *Palm trees.* Ancient name of Engedi (Gen. 14:7)

Luz. *Almond tree.* Town near ancient Bethel (Gen. 28:19; 35:6; 48:3)

Olivet. *Mount of Olives.* The hill that is before Jerusalem (1 Kings 11:7)

Rimmon. *Pomegranate.* Name assigned to a town in southern Judah (Josh. 15:32) and a city of Zebulun assigned to the Levites (1 Chron. 6:77)

Rimmon-perez. *Pomegranate of the breach.* A camping ground of the Israelites (Num. 33:19)

Rithmah. *Broom plant or juniper.* An encampment of Israel (Num. 33:21, 22)

Shamir. *Thorn.* A town in the mountains of Judah (Josh. 15:48) and one in the mountains of Ephraim (Judg. 10:1, 2)

Tamar or Thamar. *Palm tree.* A town on the southern border of Palestine (Ezek. 97:19; 48:28)

Tappuah. *Apple.* A city of Judah (Josh. 15:34)

There are also place names that refer to animals and physical features.

It is understandable why trees would be used as place names, since certain tree species found in a given location would tend to occupy the same site year after year. They would also represent landmarks for a person traveling from one location to another.

This situation is not unlike the naming of many American communities. Pineland, Buckeye, Pine Bluff, Linden, Sitka, and Lone Oak are but a few examples.

The Hebrew words "elon" or "alon" for oak, "ela" for terebinth, and "ilan" for trees are said to be remotely derived from "El," the name of God.

According to certain biblical authorities, some of the Israelite clans also had animal and plant names. The Elonites are said to be named for the oak (Num. 26:26). Among these were a Hittite, father of Bashemath (Gen. 26:34); the second of the three sons of Zebulun (Gen. 46:14) and head of the family of Elonites (Num. 26:26); and an Israelite of the tribe of Zebulun (Judg. 12:11, 12). In the geneologies of the Edomites (Gen. 36), more than one third of the clans are said to have animal names. According to tradition, they were hunters.

The clan was a group of households or an expanded family (Exod. 6:14; Num. 3:24), usually claiming a common ancestry (Gen. 24:27; 29:15; 1 Sam. 20:29). The clan was the link with the tribe (Num. 2:34).

Other interesting biblical names as they relate to plants are:

Allon—*an oak*
Bashemath—*fragrance*
Beth-haccerem—*house of the vineyard*
Carmel—*field, park, garden*
Carpus—*fruit*

Gennesaret—*garden of riches*
Gideon—*tree feller*
Ginnethon—*gardener*
Gittaim—*two winepresses*
Jipsam—*fragrant, pleasant*
Keturah—*incense*
Keziah—*cassia*
Kirjath-Jearim—*city of forests*
Koz—*a thorn*
Masrekah—*vineyard*
Mibsam—*sweet odor, balsam*
Nahalal—*pasture*
Seneh—*thorn-bush*
Suph—*reeds*

9

≉ Trees
in
Religious Worship

Ancient records reveal that trees were worshiped as gods and this is possibly the earliest form of heathen worship. Trees were thought to be the dwelling places of divine beings who were both benign and vengeful. It was assumed that if the spirits were pacified by adoration and flattery, the tree divinities would provide an abundant harvest, assure fertility to man and animal, and give success in commerce and in war. Sacrifices of food and other objects were made to the trees, accompanied by chants, such as is done today by many primitive tribes.

Early man no doubt looked upon forests as dark and foreboding. At night, as the wind blew through the leaves, or as lightning and thunder resounded through the forest, and nocturnal animals were active, the mighty voices of nature must have been evidence to early man of the existence of powerful spirits.

Heathen Worship

Among the Canaanites and other groups in Bible lands, religious worship was conducted in holy groves of trees. In the absence of groves they selected green trees with thick foliage (Ezek. 6:13; 20:28). Oak was a favorite species, (*Fig. 9–1*), as was the terebinth (Isa. 1:29, 30; 57:5). At times the poplar tree was selected as it usually remained green during the heat of the summer, especially when growing on moist sites.

Some authorities say that such wooded areas, or trees, were selected because they were places well known to the patriarchs or a place of a hero. Others believe they were selected because they protected the people from the sun as suggested by Hosea 4:13, "because the shadow thereof is good." Still others say that trees suggested life and were the abode of a spirit or divinity. Many superstitions, even to this day, are based on the latter. And, it is known that the heathen extended worship to trees, especially notable trees.

At Thebes, in the great temple of Amun (454 B.C.), oracles were given by the wind which rustled through the foliage of lofty oaks. Brazen vessels were suspended on the branches. They were blown about and came in contact with one another. Presumably the gods sent "signs" in this manner which had to be interpreted by those whose task it was to do so.

In the year 459 B.C. Scythian soothsayers used the willow as a means of divining or prophesying in the name of their gods. It was the national mode. Branches of the willow trees were cut into short pieces or rods. Each soothsayer carried large bundles of these cuttings with him. When he was asked to prophesy he placed them on the ground and shook them together. Then he placed each rod apart from the others. At this point he uttered his prediction while picking up the pieces one at a time.

Other Scythian soothsayers of this period in history used

Fig. 9–1. A large spreading oak was venerated by the heathen. Such trees were said to be the abode of divine beings. USDA

bark from the linden tree to make predictions of things to come. We more commonly know linden as the basswood. The soothsayers would remove a piece of bark from the tree and divide it into three pieces. These pieces they wound around their fingers. Prophecies would be uttered while they untwisted them.

Groves were considered as places where deity revealed itself and, in the form of oracles, made pronouncements about the future. Such groves also offered a sanctuary to common criminals and political fugitives.

In many sacred groves of trees the people performed orgiastic dances to the accompaniment of horns, drums, and cymbals as part of their religion.

Jezebel, the wife of Israel's King Ahab, built a temple to the god of the Tyrians, called Belus. Around this structure she planted a grove of all sorts of trees.

Israel was warned about making a god of the stock of a tree (Isa. 44:19) and from worshiping gods carved from the wood of cedar, cypress, oak, and ash (Isa. 44:14, 15; Jer. 2:27; Hos. 4:12).

The goddesses of fertility in Canaan, Astarte, and Anath, were worshiped principally on hills or high terrain. There the people erected Asherimor images, and set out "sacred pillars," trees under which the religious rites were practiced. As reported in the Bible: "For they also built them high places, and images, and groves, on every high hill, and under every green tree" (1 Kings 14:23). And Judah, through practicing such Canaan worship, "did evil in the sight of the Lord" (1 Kings 14:22). Also, "The children of Israel did evil in the sight of the Lord, and served Baalim" (Judg. 2:11); that is, they served Baal and Ashtaroth.

In the Old Testament, Asherah was equated with Baal and the Canaanite, the cultic symbol being the trunk of a tree with branches removed. This was a sacred pole, called Asherah.

Ezekiel reported on the faithless people who worshiped "under every thick oak" and "did offer sweet savor to all their idols" (Ezek. 6:13).

Jeremiah earnestly tried to divert the people of Judah

away from trees dedicated to lewd Asherim, of groves such as those at Byblos and Antioch in western Syria (Jer. 17:2).

It was King Ahaz of Israel, the son of Jotham, who departed from his father's ways and not only desecrated trees by making them into images but burned incense "under every green tree" (2 Chron. 28:4). For this he died at the hand of the King of Syria. At Gilgal Saul incurred the displeasure of Samuel and the judgment of God, when he offered sacrifices there to consecrate the battle against the Philistines (1 Sam. 13:4).

In ancient times in Crete and the Aegean, Zeus was considered a deity that dwelt in a sacred oak. Cedar was a venerable sacred tree and object of worship in Byblos. Sycamores, acacia, and date palms were paid similar homage in Egypt. Whatever was the precise nature of the Druids' ritual, it is known that the oak and mistletoe were venerated in their groves.

Pliny said: "The ancient ceremony of dedicating this or that kind of trees to several gods, as proper and peculiar to them, was always observed, and continues to this day. For the mighty oak, named esculus, is consecrated to Jupiter, the laurel to Apollo, the olive to Minerva, the myrtle to Venus, and the poplar to Hercules."

Ginkgo was saved from extinction because it was venerated in ancient China and cultivated in sacred groves. In Asia today a primitive tree cult holds the fig tree sacred, thus giving the scientific name *Ficus religiosa* to what is called "pipal."

It was under a fig tree in India where Gautama, father of Buddhism, received a "sense of mental clarity as to life." From under the branches of this tree he began to impart his message to all. Called the Bo Tree, it was treated with veneration by his followers until it died. A progeny of this tree was planted in Ceylon in 245 B.C. and was equally venerated.

Oak was the most highly venerated tree in Europe. An

impressive, tall, spreading tree, it was more susceptible to lightning strikes than other species. It was apparently viewed as the tree more favored by the gods of fire from heaven.

Ancient Rome (A.D. 462) had a sacred fig tree. It was located in the comitium, under which had been set an image of the she-wolf suckling Romulus and Remus, the founders of their city. The sacred area was so well-known in this historical period that a deputation from Greece, concerned with a three-year plague, came to Rome to worship and seek relief from the malady.

A sun cult in Persia pressed tree twigs to their mouths lest their breath contaminate the beneficent sun.

Likewise, respect was shown to kings and other persons of rank during the period of the Hebrew nation. Laying the hand upon the mouth implied the highest degree of reverence and submission (Job 21:5; 29:9; Ps. 39:9).

Hebrew Worship

When the Israelites settled in the Promised Land the worship of sacred trees, wells, and springs throughout the land was widespread and the custom was adopted by some Israelites, sometimes to the exclusion of Yahweh. It was, however, the Deuteronomic law to avoid worship of idols. The Hebrews were to pay homage exclusively to the one true God. Those who attempted to foment rebellion against the Lord were to be put to death (Deut. 13:1–6).

The Bible relates how Moses became angry and cast down the tables and broke them when he found the Israelites worshiping the golden calf. He took the calf, burned it and ground it into powder, scattered the ashes upon the waters, "and made the children of Israel drink of it." God forbade graven images, even the worship of trees.

Moses promulgated a code which commanded, upon entering the Promised Land, the destruction of cultic places in the mountains, hills, and under every green tree. He said, "And ye shall overthrow their altars, and break their pillars, and burn their groves with fire; and ye shall hew down the graven images of their gods, and destroy the names of them out of that place" (Deut. 12:3).

Moses desired that nothing remain to remind the Israelites of such image worship. They were even admonished not to plant "a grove of any trees near unto the altar of the Lord thy God, which thou shalt make thee" (Deut. 16:21). However, some persisted in paying homage to heathen gods.

Of the Israelites, who swore allegiance to one true God, it can be said that they lived a simple life of purity, with a strong faith in monotheism under a stringent code of ethics.

While no trees or idols made from them entered into true Hebrew worship, trees and other woody plants played a role in Jewish festivals and religious life.

For example, according to Jewish ordinances, the paschal lamb was roasted on a spit of pomegranate wood.

The Feast of Tabernacles required that they "go forth unto the mount, and fetch olive branches and pine branches, and myrtle branches, and palm branches (see *Fig. 9–2*), and branches of thick trees, to make booths, as it is written" (Neh. 8:15).

That the Jews took the Feast of the Tabernacles seriously is attested by the fact that when King Alexander stood before the altar to sacrifice, the people assembled pelted him with citrons. The reason for such action is that the Jewish law required that everyone should have branches of the palm tree and citron tree on his person during the act of worship. These the king did not have.

While the Bible does not refer to citron, Josephus refers to its use. Said he, "Upon the fifteenth day of the same month, when the season of the year is changing for winter, the law enjoins us to pitch tabernacles in every one of our houses—and keep a festival for eight days, and offer burnt-offerings, and sacrifice thank-offerings, that we should carry in our hands a branch of myrtle, and willow, and a bough of the palm-tree, with the addition of the pomecitron."

In Leviticus 23:40 reference is made to goodly trees, branches of palm trees, and boughs of thick trees and willows being used in religious services.

Other references to trees which played a role in Hebrew worship will be found throughout the book. However, under no circumstances were trees worshiped as gods.

A custom of long standing among the Hebrews was to bind together a citron bough, a sprig of myrtle, a palm branch, and willow sprigs. This bundle was then shaken toward all four cardinal points of the compass and upward and downward. The origin of the custom is shrouded in mystery.

As it pertains to the parts of the trees used in the ceremony, Jewish legend records that since the citron bough had both taste and aroma, it represents those Jews who have knowledge of the Torah and do good deeds. The myrtle has aroma but no taste and represents those who perform good deeds but do not know the Torah. The date which grows on the palm tree has taste but no aroma, thus representing those who know the Torah but do not put good deeds into practice. Lastly, the willow is without taste and aroma and represents the people who neither know the Torah nor do good deeds.

Fig. 9–2. Market in Israel selling palm branches for the lulaw during the Feast of the Tabernacles. Palm is one of the "goodly trees" mentioned in the Bible. CGI

10

🍁 Forest Workers

THE BIBLE REVEALS that there were two principal classes of forest workers. One was known as "hewers of wood," while the other was woods workers who felled trees to be made into wood products.

Hewers of Wood

The hewers of wood were gatherers of firewood, a dull and endless task. They were considered the lowest class in the listing of covenant people (Deut. 29:11). Their job was to supply the wood demands of the king and other temple requirements. That such need was great is attested by the fact that Solomon "had fourscore thousand hewers in the mountains" (1 Kings 5:15).

The Gibeonites deceived Joshua into a dishonorable peace treaty. The princes, therefore, recommended to Joshua that they be sentenced to serve as "hewers of wood and drawers of water unto all the congregation" (Josh. 9:21), a demeaning task. Said Joshua: "Now therefore you are cursed, and there shall none of you be freed from being bondmen, and hewers of wood and drawers of water for the house of my God" (Josh. 9:23).

Wood gathered by the hewers was utilized in cooking food, for heating, and for the fires which were a part of religious rites.

Hewers may properly be called slaves or servants and many of them preferred this task rather than death.

When Herodotus, the historian, visited Jerusalem, he found it difficult to induce a Hebrew to guide him on a tour of the city. His offer of gold was refused with contempt. Herodotus was an "outsider." Eventually, however, he persuaded "one of the Nethinim," hewers of wood and drawers of water to the priests and Levites, to accept his gold. The only stipulation by the hewer was that the tour be conducted at nighttime.

Nethinim was the name applied to those who were set apart to do the menial work in and around the sanctuary. The Gibeonites, first appointed as hewers of wood, became the original Nethinim.

As a result of the persecutions by Saul and the massacre at Nob, the Gibeonites were greatly reduced in numbers (1 Sam. 22:1-19). Other individuals, possibly prisoners of war who had become proselytes, were pressed into service for the Levites and were called Nethinim (1 Chron. 9:12; Ezra 2:43; 7:7; Neh. 7:46).

Presumably the Nethinim eventually merged into the Jewish population since they are not alluded to in either the Apocrypha or the New Testament.

Woods Workers

Woods workers, in contrast to hewers, were an honorable group. These were men who cut down trees to be converted into lumber and used for buildings and other products. They were a skilled group and recognized for their abilities (2 Chron. 2:8). We know these men today as "loggers" and "sawyers."

From the Bible it is known that Hiram, King of Tyre, had experts in the art of cutting down trees and hand-sawing them into lumber and other dimension materials. Solomon admitted their skill when he said, "Thou knowest that there is not among us any that can skill to hew timber like unto the Sidonians" (1 Kings 5:6).

One of the biggest timber-cutting operations recorded in the Bible resulted from a deal between Solomon and Hiram, King of Tyre (1 Kings 5:1–18). In return for an annual payment of about 125,000 bushels of wheat and 96 gallons of pure olive oil for Hiram's household, Solomon was able to secure all the cedar and cypress he needed from Hiram to build the Temple of the Lord. What an operation it must have been!

Hiram sent his tree experts to the mountains of Lebanon to cut the trees. However, they were on the payroll of Solomon who paid them good wages. In addition, Solomon drafted 30,000 men from throughout Israel to assist in the cutting and logging operation; they worked in shifts of 10,000 men, being one month in the mountains of Lebanon and two at home. Solomon's men were subordinate to the men of Tyre.

From the mountains, the woods workers brought the logs to the Mediterranean Sea where they were built into rafts, floated to Joppa, (Fig. 10–1), then taken overland to Jerusalem.

At Jerusalem the logs were cut into the desired lumber and dimension stock by Hiram's timber cutters, Solomon's draftees, and men from Gebel.

That it was an extensive long-range operation is evident from the fact that Solomon's men worked in shifts.

How the logs were skidded down the mountain to the seashore is unknown. Possibly they used animals and manpower for this task.

Fig. 10–1. Abandoned lighthouse at Joppa, on the Mediterranean. It was at this point where cedar from the forests of Lebanon was unloaded for use in the construction of Solomon's temple and for rebuilding the Temple under Zerubbabel.

Obviously Solomon produced more than a sufficient amount of lumber for the Temple alone. This was within the terms of the agreement with Hiram, however, since he told him he could have all that he desired (1 Kings 5:10).

The people of Israel, while they may not have been experts as the Sidoneans, did nonetheless cut down trees and convert the wood into the products they needed. They were encouraged to do this when they ceased to be a nomadic people and settled in more permanent abodes. As Joshua told the tribes of Joseph, "If thou be a great people, then get thee to the wood country, and cut down for thyself there . . ." (Josh. 17:15).

Tools used to cut timber and convert logs into forest products during Bible times were similar in nature to those used at the time of the founding of our nation (*Fig. 10–2*) and posed the same danger in use (Eccl. 10:9; 11:13; Isa. 10:34; 1 Chron. 20:3).

Fig. 10–2. During the early days of our nation, the method of cutting lumber, for use in construction and for other purposes, was similar to that used by the early Egyptians and others throughout the biblical period. A suspended log was cut in the approximate manner shown (courtesy American Forest Institute).

Transportation of Logs and Lumber

Solomon relied on the Phoenicians for many timber products as did other nations during this period in history. As a result, the city-kingdoms of Tyre, Byblos, Beirut, and Sidon grew rich on their skills in working metal, timber, dyeing, and the transportation of their products (Rev. 18:19).

In order to build his ships at Ezion-geber *(Fig. 10–3)*, Solomon turned to Hiram who provided his needs through the employment of 8000 camels to carry the logs to this point from the forests of Lebanon.

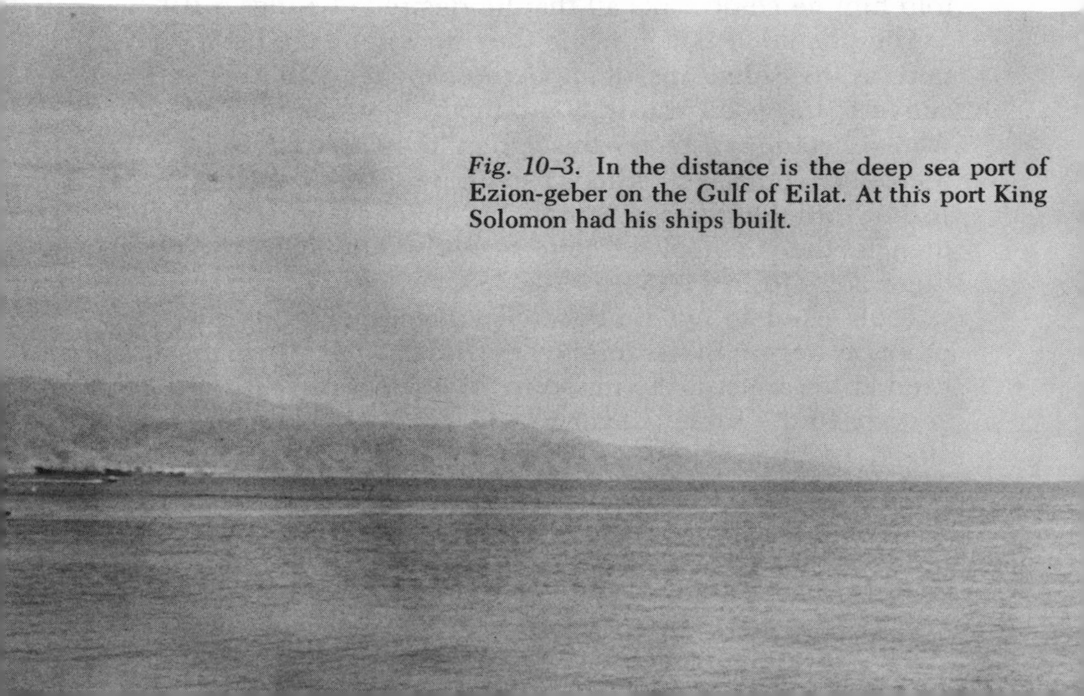

Fig. 10–3. In the distance is the deep sea port of Ezion-geber on the Gulf of Eilat. At this port King Solomon had his ships built.

Egypt and Mesopotamia had little wood to meet their needs. Memphis and Thebes to the south and Nineveh and Babylon on the east also looked to Byblos for its supply of timber. There was a great demand for wood. It was such that scarcely anything remains of the dense wooded forests which once covered the Lebanon range. Heedless cutting over the centuries, with no thought to regeneration, was principally responsible for the condition which exists to-day.

As early as 3000 B.C. ships were carrying lumber or logs, or towing logs south along the coast from Byblos to Egypt (*Fig. 10-4*). The scribe of Pharaoh Snefru left a written record that, in 2650 B.C., forty ships carrying logs or lumber were in the ports of Egypt.

The Phoenicians were people of the sea and sailed and rowed the most advanced ships of their day to the limits of the known world. Logs and timber were one of their major items of commerce.

Egypt, while a sea power, relied on other nations for its supply of wood. In 1080 B.C. when they were not a power to be feared, they sent Wen-Amun, an Egyptian envoy, to Phoenicia to secure cedar wood. It was to be used to build a sacred barge of the god Amun in Thebes. The Prince of Phoenicia was not too impressed with the envoy and agreed to supply the wood only when certain commodities he desired were delivered to him. After a period such was delivered. Said Wen-Amun in his travel diary: "In the third month of summer they dragged them down to the seashore. The Prince came out and said to me: Now, there is the last of your timber and it is ready for you. Be so good as to get it loaded up and that will not take very long. See that you get on your way and do not make the bad time of the year an excuse for remaining here."

That Egypt was an importer of wood is shown by a record in the museum at Palermo. Dated 2700 B.C., it was written by an importer in the reign of Pharaoh Snefru. Said

Fig. 10–4. Log raft on Lower Colorado River in Oregon in 1910, ready for towage to a mill in San Diego, California. Much smaller log rafts, without towage, were common along many rivers of the timbered regions of the United States during early lumbering days. This same means of transport was employed from ports near the forests of Lebanon. They were conveyed along the Mediterranean seacoasts to points as far as Egypt. This system was used to bring logs to Joppa for use in the building program of King Solomon. USFS, USDA

he: "We brought 40 ships, laden with cedar trunks. We built ships of cedarwood—one 'Pride of Two Lands,' a ship of 150 feet—and of meru wood, two ships 150 feet long. We made the doors of the King's palace of cedarwood." Meru is thought to be a coniferous species, possibly cypress.

Obviously many men were engaged in cutting and delivering logs and wood products from nations which had forest resources to others that did not.

 Workers
in
Wood

OF THE MANY ARTICLES of commerce in early biblical days, wood was one product in the greatest demand, next to food. Once the logs were cut from trees in the forest they were most generally delivered to a water port and then shipped or floated to their destination (see *Fig. 10–4*). At this point the hand sawers were responsible for cutting up the logs into the dimension of lumber needed to meet the requirements for a specific product.

Woodworkers

In early Egypt, the carpenters or woodworkers were divided into several skilled groups, each of which specialized in making specific products. Among the various crafts were the shipbuilders; basketmakers; makers of chariots and traveling carriages; cabinetmakers of can-

186

opies, palanquins, and wooden chests for traveling and religious purposes; makers of coffins; and coopers.

The work of the cooper was apparently limited since liquids were carried or kept in skins or earthenware jars. However, his skill was required to make wooden measures for grain which were bound with hoops of wood or metal.

It was necessary for each group to be skillful and conservative in the use of wood inasmuch as Egypt had little forest resources and had to import most of what they used. Timber fleets from Phoenicia brought cypress, cedar, fir, and pine to augment the meager local supply. Hardwood pegs and skillful joining made such articles strong.

Veneering, the work of Egyptian carpenters, is noted in the sculptures of Thebes as early as the time of the New Kingdom. This was about 1450 B.C.

It is evident from the records the Egyptians left that they used large quantities of wood.

Among the tools of the Egyptian carpenter were the ingenious six-foot bronze rip saws for heavy work, handsaw, axe, adz, hammer, joiner, various types of chisels, the drill, and the plane. In their work they used a ruler, a square, plummet, nails, level, nail bag, horn of oil, glue pot, and the hone (1 Chron. 20:3; Isa. 44:13; Jer. 10:4; Exod. 21:6).

Insofar as is known, the Egyptian saws were single-handed. The teeth on the saw inclined toward the hands, unlike ours today. The sawyer pulled the blade back through the wood toward himself, rather than pushing the blade as is done today. And, in most cases, they used bronze blades.

When the Hebrews left Egypt they had among them skilled workmen in wood and the other crafts as evidenced by the building of the tabernacle. When these artisans died, the arts they possessed seem to have disappeared (Judg. 5:8; 1 Sam. 13:19). This was no doubt because they were unable to work at their trade while traveling in the wilderness. Even in the time of Solomon, they needed special help from the Phoenicians (2 Sam. 5:11; 1 Kings

5:1; 7:13). However, after the era of Solomon, the craft of carpentry must have reappeared since Nebuchadnezzar II carried away carpenters among other Israelities into captivity (Jer. 24:1).

In contrast to the Egyptians, the Israelites did not have a division of work. It seems that the woodworker was a "jack of all trades," making wagons, baskets, wood carvings, and other items. Additionally, they were expert workers in stone and metal. The tools of the carpenter were similar to those used by the Egyptians.

As the Bible relates, God gave Bezalel and Oholiah, through Moses, special wisdom and skill to undertake all work necessary in the construction of the Tabernacle. He also gave these men the ability to teach others in the various crafts, including the making of boards and the carving of wood (Exod. 35:30–35).

Of interest is that the boards made for the sides of the Tabernacle were each ten cubits in length and one and one-half cubits in breadth (Exod. 26:15–16). While the width of the boards is not specified in the Bible, it may be assumed that they were about one inch in thickness due to their length. They were made from the wood of acacia trees.

A cubit is reckoned as the length of the arm from the point of the elbow to the end of the middle finger, a distance of about 18 inches. The common Hebrew cubit in early biblical days was 17.72 inches, in contrast to an Egyptian cubit of 20.67 inches.

By using these data, it should be noted that the boards ranged from about 2.2 to 2.6 feet in breadth and from 14.8 to 17.2 feet in length.

Where in the desert were acacia trees to be found that were large enough in diameter to make single boards at least 2.2 feet wide? An acacia tree would have to be about 27 inches in diameter. Length would not be a problem. It is very doubtful that acacia trees of this size were growing in the desert at the time of Moses. Trees of such size have never been a part of the desert ecology. How then did they make each board of the necessary width? Obviously, the workers were so skilled that they put smaller boards together to make one board. Perhaps they used dowels in which the Egyptians excelled. Or they may have used other means, such as a dovetail. It is of importance that, in this period of history, the Hebrews possessed great skill. All of the furnishings of the Tabernacle which they produced attest to this (Exod. 36:1–38; 37:1–29; 38:1–39; 39:1–43).

Many early kings used wood extensively in building their temples. Most prominent among these were the Etruscans who covered their buildings with rich ornamental carvings. Since they built the upper parts of wood, none of the temples remain today.

Isaiah aptly describes the work of a Babylonian carpenter who hews cedars, holm trees, oaks and ash and then converts the logs into planks. He then shapes the planks with a plane, marks them with a compass, and finally sets them in plumb with his stretched-out line (Isa. 44:13, 14).

Perhaps the best known carpenter of the Bible was Joseph, the father of Jesus (Matt. 13:55). That Jesus was also a carpenter is indicated by Mark (6:3). Like other youths in his community at Nazareth, Jesus joined his father at the carpenter's bench and helped support his family.

During his early life at Nazareth, Jesus lived at the crossroads of busy caravan routes. The Roman highways, constructed for military purposes, also put him in touch with many people. It is possible that Joseph, his father, may have been impressed into carpenter service by the Romans, as craftsmen of this period were. If so, he could have been involved in construction of public works in Nazareth, in other nearby towns, and possibly Sepphorus, the ancient capital of Galilee, or at Samaria and Jerusalem. If this was so, Jesus may have assisted his father in carpentry work at these locations.

Products of the Woodworkers

The products made by the carpenters or woodworkers were many and varied. Some have been indicated in other chapters of this book. Those named in the Bible alone would make an extensive listing.

While covered wagons may appear to be an innovation of early Americans, they were made by the carpenters and used by the princes of Israel in the desert during the time of Moses (Num. 7:3). Baskets, made of willow stems, were commonly used (Num. 6:15; Deut. 26:2, 4).

Woodworkers also made "branding irons" for merchants. In biblical times, each merchant had his own symbol or seal carved on a piece of wood about twenty inches long. It was like the branding iron of the Western range. When a merchant made a purchase, such as grain in the marketplace, he would make an impression in the soil around the grain with his seal to indicate that the product was his. Usually, in this period of history, grain was sold on the open ground.

For the tabernacle the woodworkers also crafted the altar, pillars, stays, and did the necessary wood carvings (Exod. 25:10; 26:15, 26; 35:33; 36:20, 36; 37:1, 15, 25).

Other wooden articles would include furniture, gates, pillars, jewel boxes, irrigation pumps, and structural material for homes and palaces. About 2000 B.C. the Egyptians invented locks and keys. Both of these were made from wood and were used to fasten outside doors and gates.

From many biblical references, it is obvious the manufacture of wood idols was extensive (Hab. 2:18; Rev. 9:20).

During the days of King Solomon, Egypt was the chief exporter of war chariots. The hardwood used in these swift two-wheeled chariots was imported from Syria. Egyptian chariot-makers were considered to be unsurpassed craftsmen.

For mummy cases, the woodworkers of Egypt usually used locally grown fig, but they preferred cedar from Lebanon. Cyprus, Crete, and other Mediterranean islands supplied additional needs.

Unfortunately, the poor in Bible lands did not have all the luxuries which wood provided in the way of products. Common people had little furniture. Kings had bedsteads (Deut. 3:11) and tables (Judg. 1:7). The wealthy had beds (Amos 6:4; Esther 1:6) and other luxury items.

Large wooden beams resting on stone or brick walls were the mainstay of the flat roofs of Palestine homes. Smaller beams were crisscrossed over these. Then, layers of brush, grass, reeds, mud, and clay were laid, and the clay rolled. Sycamore was used in poorer homes, while cedar and cypress were used in the homes of the more affluent. These homes usually had doors and window beams, with simple furniture (Hab. 2:11; Zeph. 2:14).

Ezekiel gives a trade inventory of imports to Palestine and its neighbors (27:4–29). Among the wood products mentioned were: ship boards of fir trees from Senir; cedar for masts from Lebanon; oaks of Bashan for oars; ebony for inlay work from many islands; and spices from Sheba and Raamah.

Wood was also dyed. Jeremiah 22:14 refers to a house "ceiled with cedar, and painted with vermilion." Varnish was used by early Egyptians on mummy cases. The varnish was made of resins taken from pine and other plants. Greeks and Romans also used varnish made from amber, mastic, and sandarac resins. The latter is from a small tree of North Africa, *Tetraclinis articulata.*

Costly scented woods were much in demand by those who could afford them (Rev. 18:2).

Early plows were direct products of a hard or dense tree. From the tree a fork or a crooked limb was cut that would suffice as a plow *(Fig. 11–1).* Eventually iron points were added to the plow.

Yokes for animals were products carefully carved from

wood and, unless properly made, imposed a burden on a work animal. Christ was well aware of this and probably helped his father make such yokes in his carpentry shop. Said he: "Take my yoke upon you, and learn of me; for I am meek and lowly in heart: and ye shall find rest unto your souls. For my yoke is easy, and my burden is light" (Matt. 11:29, 30).

For many centuries the wooden doors used in homes in the United States had the upper part in the form of a cross, symbolic of Christ's death upon the cross. He died on a cross of wood. It is interesting to note that in five scriptural passages in the New Testament, the cross is referred to as a tree (Acts 5:30; 10:39; 13:29; Gal. 3:13; 1 Peter 2:24).

It is likely that Christ, working with his father, fashioned the simple luxuries for the people of his area from wood. Such items would possibly include tables, stools, yokes, plows, saddles, and furniture. In all likehood, carpentry was Christ's full profession during the period of his life for which there is no record.

Use of Wood in Funeral Services

With a firm belief in life after death, Egyptian kings of 4600 years ago had their bodies preserved for the use of the

Workers in Wood 193

soul in the future life. They were then encased in shaped coffins made of the precious cedar of Lebanon and taken by so-called funeary boats to the site of entombment. Specialized woodworkers constructed these coffins. Some tombs contained planks of cedar shaped and prepared for assembly into heavenly barges. It was said that a departed king sailed with the sun god. Each night he vanished into the western hills and the underworld below.

Embalming had its origin in Egypt and the embalmers were so skillful that even today, after thousands of years, the features of many persons are still recognizable. Ramasses II's body, after thirty-two centuries, shows his original likeness.

The ritual of embalming took about seventy days. First, the brains were removed through the nostrils. The left flank of the body was then opened to remove the viscera. The only exception was the heart, considered then to be the seat of will and intelligence. The abdomen was cleansed with palm wine and stuffed with myrrh and cassia, the products of trees. Following this, the body was dehydrated in a natural soda, called natron. After washing and then anointing, the body was wrapped with hundreds of feet of resin-soaked linen.

Only the kings and the rich could afford the embalming process. The poor were placed in pits dug in the ground.

There are only two instances of embalming recorded in the Bible. These were Jacob and Joseph (Gen. 50:2, 26). They were embalmed to perserve their bodies for the journey to their resting place with Abraham (Gen. 50:13). It was Joseph who requested that his father be mummified.

While a coffin is referred to in Genesis 50:26, the passage is thought to refer to a mummy case. Israelites were carried on a bier to the grave. This was a flat board. The usual practice in Palestine was to bury a person a few hours after death. In some instances a body was placed in a tomb, but more frequently in a cave. The body was washed and anointed with aromatic spices (John 12:7, 19, 39).

12 ꙮꙮꙮꙮꙮꙮꙮꙮꙮꙮꙮꙮꙮ

ꙮ Forest
and
Grass Fires

MANY PASSAGES IN THE BIBLE mention forest and grass fires. Lightning was no doubt one contributing cause of fires and was common to Bible lands (Pss. 29:7; 77:17; 144:6). Man's carelessness in allowing fire to escape for malicious purposes is another. Fire was also used as a tool of warfare. How extensive fires were in Bible lands in terms of number is not known, but we do know fires occurred and did considerable damage judging by biblical records (Jer. 21:14; Ezek. 20:45–48; Prov. 30:16; Isa. 9:18; 29:6; Zech. 11:1, 2).

Samson was knowledgeable as to fire's damaging effect and used it to his advantage. It was he who tied firebrands, possibly of resinous wood, to the tails of 300 foxes. "And when he had set the brands on fire, he let them go into the standing corn of the Philistines, and burnt up both the shocks, and also the standing corn, with the vineyards and olives" (Judg. 15:4).

Absalom had his servants set fire to the field of Joab, a neighbor, merely to gel his attention to a personal problem (2 Sam. 14:30). Fires were also set to control noxious weeds (Prov. 24:31; Isa. 32:13).

Josephus reports that "fires arise of their own accord in the woods when the agitation is caused by the trees rubbing one against the other." At least, this was an assumption on his part. There is doubt that many fires were set in this manner.

Greeks and Romans are known to have used animals, including foxes, for the purpose of causing conflagrations.

Isaiah, in prophesying the destruction of Babylon, compared it to a destructive raging fire. Said he: "The fire shall burn them; they shall not deliver themselves from the power of the flame: There shall not be a coal (charcoal) to warm at, nor fire to sit before it" (Isa. 47:14).

How aptly Joel describes the effects of a devastating forest fire (Joel 1:19, 20; 2:1–10). It is an allegory in which the judgment of God takes the form of a fire. Surely Joel must have known about the destruction which fires cause, as did his listeners. Said Joel:

"O Lord, to thee will I cry: for the fire hath devoured the pastures of the wilderness, and the flame hath burned all the trees of the field. The beasts of the field cry also unto thee: for the rivers of water are dried up, and the fire hath devoured the pastures of the wilderness.

"Blow ye the trumpet in Zion, and sound an alarm in my holy mountain: let all the inhabitants of the land tremble: for the day of the Lord cometh, for it is nigh at hand. A day of darkness and of gloominess, a day of clouds and of thick darkness, as the morning spread upon the mountains: a great people and a strong; there hath not been ever the like, neither shall be any more after it, even to the years of many generations.

"A fire devoureth before them; and behind them a flame burneth: the land is as the garden of Eden before them, and behind them a desolate wilderness; yea, and nothing shall escape them. The appearance of them is as the appearance of horses; and as horsemen, so shall they run. Like the noise of chariots on the tops of mountains shall they leap, like the noise of a flame of fire that devoureth the stubble, as a strong people set in battle array. Before their face the people shall be much pained: all faces shall gather blackness.

"They shall run like mighty men; they shall climb the wall like men of war; and they shall march every one on his ways, and they shall not break their ranks: neither shall one thrust another; they shall walk every one in his path: and when they fall upon the sword, they shall not be wounded. They shall run to and fro in the city; they shall run upon the wall, they shall climb up upon the houses; they shall enter in at the windows like a thief. The earth shall quake before them; the heavens shall tremble: the sun and the moon shall be dark, and the stars shall withdraw their shining."

How vivid this description is to those who have witnessed a raging forest fire (*Fig. 12–1*) and have seen its damaging effect.

Both Isaiah and Ezekiel further describe the effects of forest, range, and field fires to relate the punishment for evil-doing and turning away from worship of God (Isa. 5:24; 9:18, 19; 10:16; 10:18, 19; Ezek. 20:47).

Punishment for one who carelessly allowed a fire to escape from his land to that of another is described in Exodus 22:6: "If a fire break out, and catch in thorns so that the stacks of corn, or the standing corn, or the field, be consumed therewith; he that kindled the fire shall surely make restitution." One who used a firebrand to start a fire was called a madman (Prov. 26:18).

The need for fire prevention is expressed in James 3:5 when it is said that a small fire kindles a large one. Fire suppression is implied in Hebrews 11:34.

Bible records indicate that fires were consuming (Deut.

Fig. 12–1. A devastating forest fire was described by Joel as one which "devoured the pastures of the wilderness, and the flame hath burned all the trees of the field" (Joel 1:19). TFS

4:24; 32:22; Obad. 1:18), burned with intensity (Zech. 12:4), were unquenchable (Jer. 7:20), roared across mountains (Ps. 83:14), and produced annoying smoke (Ps. 68:2).

Fires in the forests of Lebanon were implied in Zechariah 11:1.

Perhaps the greatest arsonist mentioned in the Bible was Abimelech (Judg. 9:46–49). While he reportedly did not set forest or grass fires, though this would not have been beneath his dignity, he and his men went to Mount Zalmon and cut green branches from trees. These they piled against the building in which the inhabitants of Shechem were and set it on fire. The building and all the people were killed by the fire and smoke. The Bible reports that about 1000 men and women lost their lives in the temple of Baal-berith. In this temple the people hoped to seek safety of their god from the vengeance of Abimelech.

Abimelech met his doom when he sought again, by arson, to burn down the wooden doors of the strong tower of Thebez. A woman threw a piece of millstone down upon him, crushing his skull. Lest it be said "a woman slew him," he had an armorbearer thrust him through with a sword and he died (Judg. 9:50–55).

While not related to forest or grass fires, there are two interesting uses of fire reported in the Bible and in the Mosaic law.

One was the Hebrew festival of the New Moon. It was a national festive day. To determine when the moon was full, watchmen were placed on commanding heights around the city of Jerusalem. When they deemed the moon full, they reported it promptly to the head of the Sanhedrin. He then declared, "It is consecrated." Immediately, word was sent throughout the land of the official pronouncement. This was accomplished by beacon fires set on the Mount of Olives (Ps. 81:3; Isa. 1:13; Ezek. 46:1; Hos. 2:11).

While we might generally associate smoke signals with Indians, it is obvious that the Hebrews were adept at this means of communication. The noted archeologist, J. L. Starkey, found letters at Lachish in 1935 that told of such signaling. Lachish was an ancient fortress of Judah. One letter contained this passage: "We are watching for the signal stations of Lachish according to all the signals you are giving because we cannot see the signals of Azekah."

An interesting parallel to fire-signaling is found in Jeremiah 6:1 where it is said: "Flee for safety, O people of Benjamin, from the midst of Jerusalem! Blow the trumpet in Tekoa, and raise a signal on Beth-haccherem; for evil looms out of the north, and great destruction."

Thus, we see trees playing a role in a joyous occasion and, unfortunately, in death.

Today, foresters and range management specialists use prescribed fires for ecological or silvicultural purposes. To the uninitiated, such fires may appear to be wild forest or range fires. However, this is not the case. Such burning is done under special climatological conditions and is regulated in such a manner as to prevent the fires from going out of control.

The practice of burning the vegetation to improve grazing conditions was used by the American Indians, among others. While such fires were not controlled as they are by scientists today, they nonetheless accomplished their objective.

Of particular interest is an historical note of about 520 B.C. pertaining to fire. According to the Periplus of Hanno account, an individual named Hanno made a voyage along the African coast southward from the Strait of Gibraltar to at least the area we know today as Liberia. As related, Hanno commanded sixty big ships. His mission was to found or regarrison certain Carthaginian stations along the Moroccan coast and southward.

In Hanno's southward exploration he and his men landed on a coastal island. This they left in panic at night after hearing the noise made by the natives and particularly after observing the sky red with fire. Further exploration along the coast revealed extensive fires which they misunderstood and feared.

What Hanno did not know was that the natives were following their usual custom of burning the dry grass at that season of the year. While this was a practice in Africa, to what extent this practice was employed in Bible lands is unknown. It is of particular interest that, during this period of history, man was sufficiently knowledgeable about fire to use it to his advantage.

13 ❧❧❧❧❧❧❧❧❧❧❧❧❧❧❧

❧ Tree
Planting

FEW REFERENCES ARE FOUND in the Bible with respect to the planting of forest trees, yet there abounds such references to fruit trees and to trees planted for special purposes, such as the production of myrrh.

Isaiah refers to the planting of ash trees "the rain doth nourish" (44:14). Abraham planted a grove in Beersheba (Gen. 21:33) which the Living Bible calls "a tamarisk tree beside the well."

One biblical passage suggests that a forest tree nursery was established: "I made me pools of water, to water therewith the wood that bringeth forth trees" (Eccl. 2:5), or as the New American Standard Version describes it: "I made me ponds of water to irrigate a forest of growing trees."

One record of tree planting was left by the scribes of King Sennacherib in 690 B.C. Wishing to be long remembered as a benefactor to his people at Nineveh, he con-

Fig. 13–1. Fruit plantation in Upper Galilee. Note cypress trees planted along road as a windbreak. Hills in background were forested in earlier biblical period. CGI

structed the first aqueduct yet discovered by archeologists in Mesopotamia. It was to provide adequate water to fulfill the people's needs. Called the Jerwan aqueduct, it was an engineering marvel.

With such volume of water available to him, King Sennacherib established a garden in which he grew cotton, myrrh, Syrian plants, fruit trees, and "trees such as grow in mountains." He even devised a swamp, and in the marsh grew fruits, vines, reeds, herbs, and forest trees. The wood from the forest trees that he grew was used in palace construction.

As reported by Josephus, Solomon had a botanical garden of trees. No doubt he had horticultural species growing in this area. It is known that he grew nut trees in the garden, and it probably contained the balsam plants as presented to Solomon by the Queen of Sheba (Song of Sol. 6:11).

From tablets found in the excavation of Sumer, evidence of afforestation is indicated. One reference is to a "grove of trees being planted to shield the garden from the withering sun and the very dry winds which carry dust from the mountains." Today we call such a planting a windbreak (Fig. 13–1).

Speaking of the Hanging Gardens of Babylon, Josephus said: "Now in this palace he erected very high walks, supported by stone pillars, and by planting what was called pensile paradise, and replenishing it with all sorts of trees, he rendered the prospect an exact resemblance of a mountain country."

That our forebears knew how to plant trees on adverse sites is reflected in the biblical passage which says that "He made him to suck oil (olive) out of flinty rock" (Deut. 32:13). Such an instance was discovered by archeologists in the arid Negeb. They came across circular stone walls in a region where there were no springs and little rainfall. When such sites were excavated they discovered the roots of ancient olive trees and vines. The stone walls, loosely

Fig. 13–2. An approximately 15-year-old stand of trees on area previously under grazing influence. Location is near Lud in Israel. For many years the government of Israel has carried on an intensive reforestation program. SL

stacked, served as a collector for valuable dew that gave moisture to the tree. The wind blowing through the rocks allowed moisture from the air to be deposited in a quantity sufficient for the early establishment of the plants.

Knowledge of the budding of trees, or the art of grafting a bud or scion of one tree onto another, was known by the Egyptians. Solomon did budding in his garden of trees, but whether this was done other than to fruit trees is unknown. It could be assumed that such a practice was carried out with nut trees, such as walnut. In Romans 11:17–24, Paul depicts God as a gardener cutting branches from one olive tree and grafting them to another olive tree. Obviously, the nature of grafting was well known to the people in his time. Rooting of tree cuttings was known and perhaps practiced (Hos. 14:5). Fruit trees, as well as horticultural species, were fertilized (Luke 13:8).

There is sufficient historical evidence to indicate that some fruit trees, such as date palm and fig, were hybridized by people in prehistoric time, though accidentally and through ignorance of the function of pollen.

Unfortunately, tree planting was not undertaken to any extent, if at all, in forested areas. Today, however, the government of Israel is carrying on an extensive reforestation program (Fig. 13–2).

14

Tree Insects and Other Depredators

TREES IN ANCIENT BIBLE LANDS were attacked by insects as they are the world over today. Such insects included bark beetles, leaf eaters, wood borers, and gall formers. A few are referred to in other chapters of this book.

Insects have been found in the fossil resin of the long extinct pine, *Pinus succinifera*.

The prophet Joel referred to armies of palmerworms, cankerworms, and caterpillars (Joel 2:25). Amos also referred to palmerworms devouring fig and olive trees, and possibly other tree species as well (Amos 4:9). Grasshoppers were also damaging but they lacked the capacity of swarming and mass migration.

Aside from insects, biblical passages relate that trees were subject to other depredations from winds, hail, fire, blights, mildew, animals, and diseases (Exod. 9:22; Ps. 29:9; 1 Kings 8:37; Rom. 8:22; Deut. 4:24; 32:22; Hag. 2:17; Jonah 4:6, 7; Hos. 5:12).

204   *Fig. 14–1.* Natives flailing, in a time-honored way, at a swarm of locusts in a futile attempt to combat them. Locusts are most damaging to field crops. They also strip the bark from trees, eat the fruit, destroy young trees, and break others by their weight. USDA

The greatest depredator of trees and other vegetation in Bible lands from the beginning of time, however, has been the locust *(Fig. 14–1)*. Locusts were most dreaded (Deut. 28:42; 1 Kings 8:37; Joel 1:4). It remains so to this day *(Fig. 14–2)*. In but a short time they can completely destroy the earnings of man's toil (Judg. 6:5; Isa. 33:4; Jer. 46:23; 51:27; Joel 2:20; Nah. 3:15).

Swarms of locusts were one of the plagues of Egypt (Exod. 10:1–20). When Pharaoh rejected the plea of Moses to let the people of Israel depart from Egypt, Moses lifted up his rod and the Lord brought an east wind which, the following day, brought the locusts. They came in dense swarms which Egypt had never experienced before or since. "They covered the face of the whole earth, so that the land was darkened; and they did eat every herb of the land, and all the fruit of the trees which the hail had left: and there remained not any green thing in the trees or in the herbs of the fields through all the land of Egypt" (Exod. 10:15).

Since the east wind blew for over a day before the plague began, this is evidence that the locusts came from a great distance. Another feature is that the plague covered all of Egypt. Ordinarily swarms would be confined to a particular area of the country. Perhaps this unusual occurrence was to prove to the Egyptians that the actions by God had no equal.

Only in response to Pharaoh's plea "the Lord turned a mighty strong west wind, which took away the locusts and cast them into the Red sea" (Exod. 10:19).

Locusts, when they swarm, devour everything in their path which is green. They strip the bark from forest and fruit trees and other woody vegetation, eat the fruit, destroy young trees, and break others by their weight. Biblical records relate their destructiveness (Exod. 10:12–19; Joel 1:4, 7, 10, 12, 16, 18, 20; 2:3). They breed every six weeks on their devastating migration.

Particularly are the locusts damaging to field crops and grazing lands, and when this occurs, it creates destitution among the people. There is no grain for food, nor grazing for the animals. And famine means death.

It has been reported that a swarm of locusts one mile square will eat 400 tons of grain each day, attesting the damage this insect can bring to green plants. It is also known that this insect can devour all vegetation on a 100-square-mile area in one day. No doubt the prophets were aware of this damage.

The accompanying map *(Fig. 14–2)* shows the breeding areas and principal migration routes of the insect today. No doubt this pattern has been consistent over the centuries. It is of interest to conjecture where the locust plague of Egypt had its origin.

The Bible does point out the destructive nature of locusts and the powerlessness of man to combat them.

Moist soil conditions, a large amount of vegetation, and strong winds are among the factors that seem to favor their spread.

Fig. 14–3. A dense swarm of locusts that darkens the sky. Today, planes are used to spray the insect to bring about some control over them. USDA

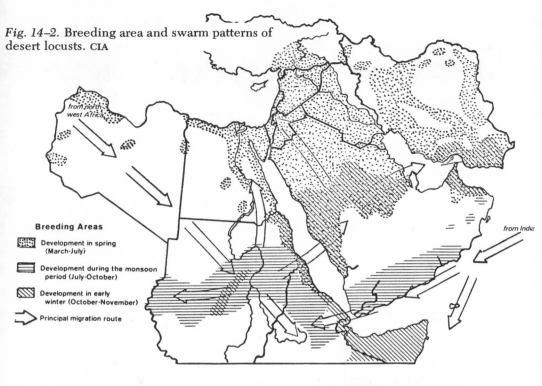

Fig. 14–2. Breeding area and swarm patterns of desert locusts. CIA

Breeding Areas

- Development in spring (March-July)
- Development during the monsoon period (July-October)
- Development in early winter (October-November)
- Principal migration route

from north-west Africa

from India

They fly in the direction of the wind (Prov. 30:27; Nah. 3:16, 17), travel in large numbers (Jer. 46:23), and swarm as to darken the land (Joel 2:2, 10; Exod. 10:15). They make a noise with their wings when in flight (Joel 2:2), and if dew is on the ground they wait to be warmed by the sun before going further (Nah. 3:17). Locusts even enter the doors and windows of poorly constructed homes (Joel 2:7–9).

Even today the locusts are difficult to control despite the intensive campaigns against them (Fig. 14–3).

15 🍁🍁🍁🍁🍁🍁🍁🍁🍁🍁🍁🍁🍁🍁

🍁 Shipping
and
Shipbuilding

Shipbuilding

Within the Fertile Crescent *(Fig. 3–8)* there were three major bodies of water, represented today as the Red and Mediterranean Seas and the Persian Gulf. These, with the navigable rivers and lakes, mandated that ships and boats be employed as a means of transportation for commerce and other purposes. Unfortunately, many ships were extensively used for warfare.

Thus, at an early stage in man's progress, shipbuilding was of vital importance and became increasingly so as the centuries went by.

Originally, vessels with sails were the ones primarily built. Since such ships could lie becalmed for days, ships were constructed that used oars as the means of navigation when calms prevailed.

208   Fig. 15–1. Vast quantities of wood were needed for vessels of war in ancient periods. In the war between the Romans and Carthaginians, more than 700 ships were launched. Sails and oars were used to maneuver the ships (sketch courtesy the U.S. Department of the Navy).

There are no biblical records, except one, concerning successful shipyards or the extent of shipbuilding other than to point out that ships and boats were extensively used. The one exception is Solomon's shipyard.

King Jehoshaphat of Judaea did join with King Ahaziah of Israel to build ships at Ezion-geber. Their plan was to go to Ophir for gold. Because of their poor construction the ships capsized at the port and the project was given up. Eliezer, the prophet, had prophesied such would occur (1 Kings 22:48; 2 Chron. 20:35).

Wood was the only product used for boat construction and such usage continued through the 1600s. Obviously, large quantities were required during the biblical period and this demand put a drain on the forest resources of the then known world.

There seems to be little doubt that Egypt had the first shipbuilders. The Phoenicians, however, were a close second. Seafaring occupations were prominent in the great empires of the Nile, Tigris-Euphrates, and Phoenician coastal cities in early biblical history.

Extensive quantities of wood were used for war vessels. At the great battle of Ecnomus (256 B.C.) between the Romans and Carthaginians, said by some to have been the greatest naval engagement of antiquity, *(Fig. 15–1),* be-

tween 700 and 800 big ships were engaged. It is evident
that these nations had active shipbuilding programs.

In 262 B.C. the ruling type of battleship was the trireme,
a galley with three bands of oars. At this period the Carthaginians developed a quinquereme, with a much bigger
galley employing five banks of oars. It could ram or shear
the oars of any smaller ship.

Obviously, shipbuilding for war vessels alone in this
period of history was important.

Before the nineteenth century no ships were built any-
where in the world that exceeded 2000 tons burden.

Shipping

In Egypt, flat bottom wooden boats were constructed for
use in fishing and hunting in the delta marshes. Many are
reported to have been made from acacia wood. Large
barges were made to transport stone from Upper Egypt.
Also, trading boats plied the river and seas, and special
funeral barges were constructed. Since Egypt had little
tree resources, the wood for shipbuilding had to be imported. As early as 2500 B.C. Egyptians launched merchant
vessels as much as 100 feet in length.

One Egyptian record of about 3000 B.C. referred to "Byblos ships" that bore cedars of Lebanon to their country. It is
known that the Babylonians were sailing ships of commerce to India about 3000 B.C.

From an existing record it is noted that, in 1500 B.C.,
Queen Hatshepsut of Egypt sent out a fleet of five wooden
ships to Punt. They went to reestablish trade interrupted
by the Hykos wars, and with orders to bring back myrrh
trees for the temple terrace. When they returned they had a
cargo of myrrh trees, ebony, gold, sweet-smelling wood,
sandalwood, panther skins, and apes.

An interesting account is given of Thutmose III, an
Egyptian king who conquered Palestine, Syria, and
Phoenicia in the fifteenth century B.C. He commanded that
strong boats of cedar be built behind the Lebanese coast

and carried on carts as far as the Euphrates. What an engineering feat this must have been.

The Hebrews were not a seafaring people. Neither were they merchants in terms of travel. Rather, they were middlemen. Yet, drawings of ships in ancient Jewish tombs indicate an interest in maritime commerce. Solomon did operate a fleet of ore ships from Ezion-geber about 960 B.C., but these were manned principally by Phoenicians. Ezion-geber is known today as Tel el Kheleifeh.

Solomon's main income did not come from taxes upon the people but from the traffic of merchants and merchant seamen. Some historians suggest that the visit of the Queen of Sheba to Jerusalem was a diplomatic mission relating to the expansion of Israel's trade routes at the expense of other nations.

The Bible does indicate that the tribe of Dan apparently had ships (Judg. 5:17).

The Phoenicians had a reputation for shipbuilding and navigational skills. The larger ships, made from cypress, had cedar masts, fir flooring, oak oars, and boxwood rowing benches. During the period of 900 to 600 B.C. the Phoenicians were at their zenith (Isa. 23:8) and are known to have traded as far as the Azores in the mid-Atlantic.

Phoenicians were so skilled in seamanship that they lashed huge logs together and floated them south of the Mediterranean without using any cargo vessels. Their principal trade ships had long galleys with fifty oars, and a crew well armed and ready for fighting.

The Greeks were also great shipbuilders and had trading posts in Egypt in 650 B.C., as well as among the islands of the Aegean, and the Black and Ionian seas. Greek commerce included wood products along with their famous Greek pottery, oils, wines, and honey. From the third century B.C. Greek freighters ten times the size of the *Santa Maria* could carry 200 tons.

Records show that in 14 B.C. the king of Cyprus sent letters to the kings and other rulers throughout the region offering to ship copper and wood in return for such items as silver, oil, and manufactured goods.

Many types of boats were constructed by those who lived along navigable water courses and lakes in biblical times. A ferry boat was used to carry King David and his household over the Jordan River (2 Sam. 19:16–18). Jesus crossed the Sea of Galilee in a small fishing boat. Paul traveled extensively by ship and was involved in a shipwreck in which he foretold that there would be no loss of life but that the ship would be destroyed (Acts 27:22). According to biblical authorities this was a large merchant ship and carried 276 persons (Acts 27:37).

There were no large passenger boats as such during the biblical period. Primarily they were either warships or merchant vessels which carried passengers as a sideline. Merchant vessels depended upon sails, whereas warships depended upon sails and oars, the latter so that they could better maneuver the vessel in battle. In 31 B.C. warships of moderate size were about 100 feet in length and displaced about 81 tons. Each vessel had 180 rowers, 25 mariners, and 80 soldiers.

According to available records many merchant vessels in 1 B.C. exceeded 100 feet in length. Some were 180 feet in length.

It is interesting to note that, in 1620, the frail wooden boat which brought the Pilgrims to our shores was only 92 feet in length (*Fig. 15–2*).

Solomon's Shipyard

"And King Solomon made a navy of ships in Eziongeber, which is beside Eloth, on the shore of the Red Sea, in the land of Edom" (1 Kings 9:26). At this period in biblical history Edom reached down to the gulf of the Red Sea. The trees in the high mountains of Edom apparently could not supply Solomon's need for construction purposes.

Where, then, did the wood come from to construct the large vessels of trade? Ezion-geber had only palm trees.

Fig. 15–2. Replica of the historic *Mayflower* which brought the Pilgrims to the shores of America. Made of wood, it was only about 92 feet in length (photo courtesy Massachusetts Department of Environmental Management).

King Solomon made a contract with Hiram, King of Tyre, to provide the wood he needed, not only for the ships but for other building purposes as well. In return for this Hiram was given the village and port of Eilotha.

A record by a Phoenician priest said: "Although there were great palm forests in the neighborhood of this place, there was no suitable timber for building purposes, so Hiram had to transport the timber there on 8000 camels." What a transportation problem this must have been considering the amount and size of wood needed! Over 270 miles of rugged desert separated the supply source from the point of manufacture.

Solomon built ten ships from the wood delivered. Once every three years his ships made the trip to Ophir to distribute his copper and bring back cargoes of gold, algum trees, and other items (1 Kings 9:26–28). While Ophir has never been properly located, it is thought Solomon may have had trade with Africa and perhaps Punt, based on products he received in return for his ore and other goods.

Recently scientists with the U.S. Geological Survey reported that Mahd adh Dhahab, midway between Mecca and Madina in Saudi Arabia, may have been the biblical "Ophir" that sustained Solomon's wealth. They say that this area was rich enough in gold and a convenient location to qualify. The scientists also stated that the area lies on a natural trade route some 600 miles from Ezion-geber, a long but feasible journey.

Concerning the land of Ophir Josephus said, "Solomon gave this command: That they (Phoenicians) should go along with his own stewards to the land that was of old called Ophir, but now Aurea Chersonesus, which belongs to India, to fetch him gold." He further stated: "King Solomon received from Aurea Chersonesus, pine trees, used for supporting the temple and the palace and for musical instruments. They were larger and finer than any that had been brought before—like the wood of a fig tree, but whiter and more shiny."

The Bible does not record whether or not the ten ships under Solomon's command remained in service over any lengthy period. An interesting report on one of them is given by Cyrus H. Gordon of the Department of Mediterranean Studies at Brandeis University based on stone markings found in the tropical rain forest of Paraiba, in the country of Brazil. The inscription, translated by Gordon, follows: "We are Sidonian Canaanites from the city of the Mercantile King. We were cast upon this distant shore, a land of mountains. We sacrificed a youth to the celestial gods and goddesses in the nineteenth year of our mighty King Hiram and embarked from Ezion-geber into the Red Sea. We voyaged with ten ships and were at sea together for two years around Africa. Then we were separated by the hand of Baal and were no longer with our companions. So we have come here, twelve men and three women, into New Shore. Am I, the Admiral, a man who would flee? Nay! May the celestial gods and goddesses favor us well."

Evidently Solomon's fleet of ten ships traveled extensively throughout the then known world.

Since early in his history man has used the stars to guide him in his voyages. Such was the case during the Bible period. The compass was first used at sea by Seig B. Givaia, of Naples, in the thirteenth century.

The Ark

Perhaps the greatest shipbuilding feat in history, considering the era in which it was constructed, was the three-storied ark *(Fig. 15–3)* built by Noah at God's command (Gen. 6:14–17).

Measurements as to its dimensions are given in the Bible in cubits. While the exact length of a cubit is unknown, 18 inches is generally accepted by many authorities. Using this unit of measurement, we note that Noah built a wooden ship 450 feet in length, 75 feet in width, 45 feet in height and with volume capacity of over 1.5 million cubic feet. By displacement standards, the ark was a ship of about 66,000 tons.

Fig. 15–3. An artist's conception of the three-storied ark built by Noah at God's command (courtesy Creation Science Research Center).

Not until the nineteenth century was there built a boat that exceeded it in length. The great *Easter*, the ship that laid the North Atlantic transcontinental cable, was 628 feet in length, 83 feet wide and 58 feet in height. It was built in 1858.

Obviously, there existed skilled woodworkers in that ancient period whose knowledge was not equaled until recent times. The construction of the ark was a mammoth undertaking that must have employed hundreds of people.

A ship of this size would require a large keel or central rib to support the massive weight. This had to be constructed from many pieces of quality wood laminated skillfully together with precision. The ribbing would have to be similarly constructed, as would other parts of the ark. It was an engineering marvel.

History does not record where the gopher wood came from to build the ark. Quality, long stemmed trees would be needed. Some speculate, however, that the wood resource might have been available locally in that period of history. They speculate further that the ark was probably built near the Tigris River and that the gopher wood was likely an oak from the white oak family. Authorities generally agree that the gopher wood Noah referred to was most likely cypress, in which case it may have been necessary to import the wood from a distant point. What a transportation problem this would have presented!

Noah must have been a man of wealth to afford the overall costs incurred in building such a ship. He had to be a man of experience as well. Above all, Noah was a man of strong faith.

It is conservatively estimated that about 650,000 board feet of lumber were used by Noah in the ark's construction.

16

☙ Apothecaries

THE APOTHECARIES OF EARLY BIBLE times were men of stature in their cities and were held in considerable esteem, as were physicians. It might be said that they were the botanists of their period. Most knowledgeable about trees and other plants, they compounded and sold sweet spices and anointing oils. They were also perfumers and dispensed cosmetics, perfumes, scents of attar of roses, incense for temples, rose water and violet essence for candy flavoring, licorice water, and plants for medicine and seasoning.

All large cities in the early Bible period had a perfumer's street where the apothecaries compounded the drugs, oils, and perfumes of their trade. Their stock included all known fragrant substances in the form of powder, compressed cake, essence of spirit, oil, fat, seeds, leaves, and bark.

In a clay tablet found in Nippur, dated 2600 B.C., there is a prescription for the treatment of a man burned "from things in a furnace." It said: "Put on balsam potion made of barley, salt and cassia." It also called for "plaster on the leg and an anointing with barley beer and hot water, sesame, and cedar oil," all substances provided by the apothecaries.

The Bible is rich in allusions to trees, herbs, and spicy plants used for culinary, medicinal, cosmetic, prophylatic, and worship purposes.

No doubt the Israelites cultivated a desire for perfumes, unguents, incense, and other products of the apothecary during their sojourn in Egypt. Later they feared when invaders came into their country lest their daughters be carried off to become perfumers (1 Sam. 8:13).

Perhaps Bezaleel could be called the first biblical druggist since he compounded the first anointing oil (Exod. 31:11; 37:29).

Of importance in the act of the ancient apothecary was the mixing of medicinal herbs. Babylonia and Egypt were among the early nations that developed the medical art of the apothecary.

Apothecaries were also responsible for preparing spices for burials (2 Chron. 16:14).

17

✲ Dresser of the Sycamore

"I AM NO PROPHET, nor a prophet's son; but I am a herdsman, and a dresser of sycamore trees" (Amos 7:14 RSV.). These were the words of Amos, from the region of Tekoa, about ten miles south of Jerusalem, in the mountain pasture land overlooking Judaea.

Obviously Amos, in addition to carrying on his herdsman's duties with cattle, also indulged in the sideline of "dressing" fig trees.

The King James Version says he was a "gatherer of sycamore fruit"; but there is generally agreement among biblical scholars that his activity involved more than merely gathering the fruit. Whether Amos was involved in "dressing" the sycamore fruit for his own use and benefit or as a vocation in which he helped others is not indicated in the Scripture. Yet, the implication is that it was a vocation or occupation which he pursued.

Biblical Translation of "Dresser"

There is a question as to the interpretation of the word "dresser." In the Hebrew version of the Bible, the activity associated with Amos is given as "Boless Shikmim." The word "Shikma" is sycamore; however, the word "Boless" appears but once in the Bible and its meaning is not clear. In the Septuagint, the well-known Greek translation of the Bible made in Alexandria about 200 B.C., "Boless Shikmim" is translated as "Knizon Sycamina," a "piercer of sycamore figs." Authorities agree that "grower" or "gatherer" has no application to the interpretation of both sources, and that Amos was involved in some special activity.

The Sycamore Fig

The sycamore to which Amos had reference is a fig, *Ficus sycamorus,* which grew wild over an extensive region. It is found wherever there is a spot of fertile soil, from the mountains of Lebanon to the Dead Sea. It is a tree with a leaf looking somewhat like a mulberry leaf and is also known as a mulberry fig. Both fig and mulberry belong to the same plant family.

Up to six crops of fruit may be produced in one year by a single tree.

According to some scientists the sycamore fig had its origin in the savannas of Central Africa and Yemen *(Fig. 17–1).* In these locations the fruit produces viable seed. A small wasp, *Ceratosolen arabicus,* is responsible for the necessary pollination. If this fig had its origin as speculated, the spread of the species by man or nature must have taken place at an early point in history since the tree was established in the biblical lands in Bible times.

It is known that the sycamore fig growing in the Holy Land, Egypt, and Cyprus produces no viable seed and may well be different varieties. In each location, however, a fig wasp is present that does extensive damage to the fruit.

Fig. 17–1. A wild fig growing out of a crack in a solid rock in the Union of South Africa. Scientists say that the sycamore fig of the Bible lands had its origin in the savannas of Central Africa. This wild fig will be found growing in its native area where there is a spot of fertile soil. USDA

The female wasp deposits her eggs into the ovaries of the female fig flowers and the fig becomes infested with larvae. Apparently the wasps are not effective enough in pollination to produce viable seeds.

The sycamore is a fig of poor quality, much inferior to the common fig, and the tree grows to a height of about thirty feet. Its fruit is inferior in taste and has a much lower sugar content. It was extensively eaten by the poor who could not afford the more expensive fruits.

The importance of this fig in the Bible is attested by King David's appointment of overseers for trees in the Shephelah (1 Chron. 27:28; Ps. 78:47; Isa. 9:10; Hos. 9:9). Its abundance in Bible times is suggested by references in 1 Kings 10:27, 2 Chronicles 1:15 and 9:27.

Dressing of Figs

What was the nature of Amos' "dressing" of the figs? Biblical writers have varied opinions. Among those cited are: the operation of cutting the top of each fig to insure ripening; to puncture unripe fruit to make it more edible and, therefore, saleable; to open the fruit to get rid of the insects that infest it; to pinch the fruit; the process of pruning or nipping back the trees for better yields of fruit; and the puncturing or piercing of premature fruit with a nail or other sharp instrument to accelerate ripening.

From historical records the practice of gashing or piercing immature sycamore figs to induce ripening can be traced back to early Egyptian civilizations. Gashed figs have been found in tombs or depicted on bas-reliefs dating as early as 1100 B.C. Theophrastus (372–287 B.C.) stated that the sycamore fig "cannot ripen unless it is scraped, but they scrape it with iron claws, the fruit thus scraped ripens in four days."

The scraping of immature figs to induce their ripening without the help of cross pollination is still practiced in Egypt, Turkey, and Cyprus today. The scraping consists of making a slight cut on the small, hard green figs with a kitchen knife or some such tool. No specific area need be cut. Rather, such a cut is made hurriedly at random. In Cyprus today the only way to obtain edible fruit is by gashing.

The gashing so applied to the small fruit induces speedy growth and in three or four days the figs increase about seven times in weight and volume.

Generally the gashing takes place before the small figs are susceptible to infestation by wasps. It produces edible fruit free of insects. If some infestation has occurred, the insects inside the fruit do not develop to cause any harm and the fruit is edible. Gashing is usually done when the fruit is about sixteen days old.

Evidently Amos was well aware of the gashing techniques for fig development and put his art into practice while he cared for his livestock.

18

⁂⁂⁂⁂⁂⁂⁂⁂⁂⁂⁂⁂⁂⁂

⁂ The
Condemned
Tree

OF ALL THE TREES MENTIONED in the Bible one, a fig tree, was condemned to die as an object lesson to Christ's disciples. To quote the scriptural account: "And seeing a fig tree afar off having leaves, he came, if haply he might find any thing thereon: and when he came to it, he found nothing but leaves; for the time of figs was not yet. And Jesus answered and said unto it, No man eat fruit of thee hereafter for ever. And his disciples heard it" (Mark 11:13, 14).

The following morning as Christ and his disciples passed the tree the disciples noted that the fig tree had dried up and was dead. "And Peter calling to remembrance saith unto him, Master, behold the fig tree which thou cursedst is withered away. And Jesus answering saith unto them, Have faith in God" (Mark 11:21, 22).

Of biological interest is that portion of the biblical account that says "for the time of figs was not yet." It is evident, therefore, that Christ did not expect ripe fruit. Possibly the time of the event was two months prior to around June when the fruit matures.

Probably Christ did expect to find undeveloped but edible fruit buds on the tree to appease his hunger (Mark 11:12). Since there was no undeveloped fruit, it was obvious that the tree would not produce a crop of figs in the summer. Thus, he condemned the tree as an object lesson to his followers to "bring forth fruit" in their personal lives (John 15:16).

In his action, Christ reiterated the principle he often stated that "every tree that bringeth not forth good fruit is hewn down, and cast into the fire" (Matt. 7:19). "Why cumbereth it the ground?" he also asked (Luke 13:7).

It was the practice in biblical lands to cut down and destroy trees that did not bear fruit after three years. In this way they practiced a form of plant selection, even as we do today.

19

Products of Trees and Other Woody Plants

MANY REFERENCES ARE FOUND in the Bible concerning contributions made to man by products of trees and woody plants since the beginning of time. Some references, such as the use of charcoal, come by inference while others are specific. Other supplemental information to the Bible period is revealed by historical records left by past civilizations.

In addition to providing man's basic demands for food, clothing, and shelter, woody plants met many other social and economic needs. Without charcoal, a product of the tree, man could not have produced iron and copper from the ore in the mountains. Woody plants helped provide his medical needs and supplied the tannin to produce leather. Products from others were used for dyeing clothing, in writing inks, in beverages, and for many other uses.

Some products have been discussed in earlier chapters. A discussion of others follows.

Beverages

Root beer may appear to be an innovation of the Americans. Yet such a commodity was exported by Babylon. Made of an extract of tree, shrub, and other plant roots, it could be kept for long periods in the climate of biblical lands. To make the beverage, all one had to do was add water.

Wine was made from the fruit of the pomegranate (Song of Sol. 8:2) and from the fruits of other trees. Pliny left a record that the carob tree fruit was similarly used.

Scented waters were made by confectioners, female perfumers or apothecaries (1 Sam. 8:13). These waters were kept in large sealed bottles for use in the summer as cooling syrup drinks. Such waters were made when orange trees, violets, and roses were in bloom.

Charcoal

There is no direct reference to charcoal in the King James Version of the Bible. The references are to "coal" or "coals." These do not refer to coal as we know it, inasmuch as this substance was not then known in Palestine or in other areas of Bible lands. Rather, the passages refer to charcoal or live embers of other combustible substances. Man learned at an early date that charcoal has twice the heating power of wood and burns without flame and smoke. He learned also that the best yields of charcoal came from denser hardwoods, such as oak.

An early use of charcoal was reported by Parrot, a well-known archeologist, in his excavation of the site of the mighty capitol of the Kingdom of Mari. This kingdom was destroyed in 1700 B.C. Parrot found charcoal in the ovens of the king's kitchen. This kingdom included the Haran of the Bible, the home of Abraham. The inhabitants of Mari were Amorites.

Since the beginning of time, charcoal has been widely used. The Hebrews used it for heating or cooking (John 18:18; 21:9). However, wood, dried grass, dung of camels, and various thorn bushes were used for fuel as well (Isa. 9:15; Ezek. 4:13, 15; 15:4, 6; 21:32). Homes of the Israelites in Bible times did not have chimneys. There was a hole in the roof through which smoke escaped. In the poorer families wood was used as fuel. In the wealthier homes the rooms were warmed by charcoal in braziers (Jer. 36:22; Mark 14:54; John 18:18).

The Bible indicates that food was cooked in a variety of ways, namely with charcoal (Prov. 26:21), thorns (Isa. 33:12), sticks (1 Kings 17:10) or grass (Luke 12:28).

The greatest consumption of charcoal was no doubt involved in the reducing and fashioning of metals. The charcoal-smudged Phoenician metalsmiths beat out copper, bronze, and iron weapons for which they were renowned. The Hebrews were knowledgeable in this craft as well.

The origin of charcoal is unknown, but early man soon found that he could cook with it inside his abode without the danger of sparks and the annoyance of irritating smoke. Nor did the fuel flame—it merely glowed.

In the production of charcoal, the impurities of the wood are driven off, leaving only the carbon. This is accomplished by stacking wood, setting it on fire, and then covering it with soil. Most of the air is kept away, thus forcing the fire to burn slowly. The time when the charcoal was ready for use was determined by the color and amount of smoke in the burning process.

Some tree species are better suited than others for charcoal production, and oak has always been the favorite. Best yields are obtained from the denser woods, such as oak, hickory, and beech. In the process of destructive distillation, yield per cord is about forty-five bushels.

During the days of the Roman Empire charcoal was extensively used for heating homes, for metal forging, and in street lighting.

England built her iron industry on the use of charcoal, and so much oak and other hardwoods were used that it contributed to the denudation of Britain's forest resources.

It was before a warming charcoal fire on a cold night that Simon Peter denied knowing Christ (John 18:17, 18).

Vast amounts of charcoal were used in Bible days for smelting. When King David conquered Edom the victory was of economic significance. The Arabah desert, which stretches from the southern end of the Dead Sea to the Gulf of Aqabah, was rich in iron and copper. David needed iron since, in this period of history, the Philistines had a monopoly on the metal (1 Sam. 3:19, 20). "And David prepared iron in abundance for the nails for the doors of the gates, and for the joinings: and brass in abundance without weight" (1 Chron. 22:3).

It was King Solomon, however, who followed up the full commercial opportunities that this conquest provided.

Evidently, both Solomon and David were aware of the rich iron and copper potential in this area from previous mining operations by the Egyptians. Such is the opinion of Israeli archeologist Beno Rothenberg who states that the mines were in operation as early as 1406 B.C., producing copper ingots 97 to 98 percent pure. His view is that the mines were built by Egypt's pharaohs of the nineteenth and twentieth dynasties. Perhaps, as he suggested, the Egyptians borrowed the metallurgical techniques from the Midianites who lived in the area and are referred to in Genesis as the first metal workers.

Solomon built a major smelting and refining center at Ezion-geber, at the head of the Gulf of Aqabah. Actually, he constructed a number of smelting centers down the great desert rift of the Wadi Arabah, between the southern end of the Dead Sea to the Gulf. This divided Palestine from Transjordan. These smelters produced the metal for ritual furnishings for the Temple, including the two great pillars, Jachin and Boaz, in the porch of the Temple (1 Kings 7:15; 2 Chron. 4).

Ezion-geber had wells of sweet water and oasis palms that provided shelter and food. The smelter and refining center at Ezion-geber was at a point on the shore where drafts up the Wadi provided air for the smelting process. The refined copper was used by Solomon but it was also an important item of commerce. From Ezion-geber ships went to southern Arabia, Egypt, and Sinai transporting copper and other products, returning with spices, gums, gems, and other items.

Credit for exploration that led to the discovery of King Solomon's mines, forts, and seaports at Ezion-geber is due the famous archeologist, Dr. Nelson Glueck.

Up to the middle of the eighteenth century, iron continued to be reduced from ores by means of wood charcoal. The iron was handled in small pieces, and hammered and wrought into shape by skilled craftsmen.

Though not mentioned in the Bible, huge quantities of charcoal, principally from oaks and other hardwood species, were needed for Solomon's extensive refinery fires. Since Ezion-geber was located in a region with but few scrubby hardwoods, it was necessary to secure the needed product over an extensive area. One record indicates that charcoal from the forests of Edom was used. Still another says that acacia charcoal was used. An additional record shows that King Hiram also provided charcoal. King David possibly secured his supplies from the same source.

Cosmetics

Milady, from the beginning of time, has used the products of trees, among other plants, for beautification purposes. Cosmetics were common in Egypt and Ur as early as 3000 B.C.

Jezebel used such beauty aids on her skin and hair (2 Kings 9:30). Use of eye shadow was a common practice

(Ezek. 23:40) as was face powder (Jer. 4:30). Even, black, heavy lines were made under the eyes to make them look larger.

Unguents and perfumes were also used in garments (Ps. 45:8; Song of Sol. 3:6), and hair sets were common (Isa. 3:24).

While we may look upon false hair as being an innovation of Americans, it was common in biblical times.

Toes, fingernails, and hair were tinted then, as now, with henna plant juice. Charcoal, finely ground, was used as an eye shadow. Galena was used to tint eyebrows and eyelashes. For lipstick these early beauticians used insects to provide the carmine such as is done today. In the cosmetic trade it is known as Carmine N.F. Derived from cochineal, it is made from the dried bodies of the females of certain scaly insects.

Cosmetics, especially among the wealthy, were kept in toilet boxes made of ivory, ebony, or other precious woods. Wooden sticks were among the utensils used to apply material to the eyes.

Dyes

Trees played a role in producing some of the dyes used by man over the centuries. The dyeing of textiles was in existence many years before Abraham. Dyeing vats have been excavated at Lachish to prove this. That dyes were known in an early period is related in the story of the birth of Zarah with the identifying first-born scarlet thread "upon his hand" (Gen. 38:28, 30). Moses prepared curtains for use in the tabernacle using dyes of blue, purple, and scarlet (Exod. 26:1).

While the Bible does not refer to a professional group of dyers, excavations have revealed that a guild of dyers existed in the vicinity of Thyatira. Luke did refer to a woman by the name of Lydia, a seller of purple in the city of Thyatira (Acts 16:14). Apparently, in most instances, the dyers were also weavers.

The people of Israel liked bright colors. It extended to their dress, the walls of their homes, and the faces of the women. Joseph was given a coat of many colors (Gen. 37:3). Red and blue seems to have been reserved for men's wear and green for women. During the Hebrew wandering in the desert, blue, purple, and scarlet dyes are mentioned as offerings to Moses by the people (Exod. 25:4). "Ye daughters of Israel, weep over Saul who clothed you in scarlet" (2 Sam. 1:24), said David in his grief for the first king. The king's virgin daughters were clothed with "a garment of divers colors" (2 Sam. 13:18).

Of the various colors used for dyeing purposes in ancient times, the bark of the pomegranate tree supplied black, while almond leaves yielded yellow. Indigo came from the rind of the pomegranate. Potash, lime, and grape treacle also yielded blue.

Deep red, crimson or scarlet was obtained from a small insect, *Coccus ilicis,* which drew its nourishment from the leaves of an oak. The insect was called "Kirmiz" by the Arabs, from which the English word "crimson" was derived. It was from the eggs of the female grub that the coloring matter was derived.

Blue came principally from a shellfish, *Helix Ianthina,* which was apparently more violet in color. Another shellfish, a small mollusk, *Murex trunculus,* produced purple. It was a secretion obtained from a small gland, the fluid of which is at first whitish, but changes to purple on exposure to sunlight. The oldest site of the purple trade was Tyre. Purple was a costly dye and the Phoenicians were expert in its production. Because of its cost it became a mark of distinction to wear a robe of this color (Jer. 14:4). Early royalty were so robed and in later periods ecclesiastical officials also so arrayed themselves.

Robes of scarlet, probably a rich crimson, were worn by the rich. It was expensive apparel in biblical times (2 Sam. 1:24; Prov. 31:21; Lam. 4:5; Rev. 17:4). Scarlet cloth was used for the hangings in the tabernacle (Exod. 25:4; Num.

4:8) and for priestly vestments (Exod. 39:1). In Song of Solomon 4:3, the lips of a bride are likened to a scarlet thread. A scarlet robe was placed on Christ by the soldiers in Pilate's judgment hall (Matt. 27:28).

Vermilion was used as a paint for the inside of a home (Jer. 22:14).

In the dyeing of cloth the dyers generally tinted threads instead of the cloth because the people favored multicolored garments.

Greeks called the manufacturers of purple "purple dyers" or "Phoenicia," which meant purple in their language. Few plant dyes are used today. They have been supplanted by synthetics which are cheaper and can produce a wider range of colors.

Garlands and Wreaths

It was the custom in heathen sacrifices to adorn the victims with garlands around the neck and fillets around the head. These were made up of the small branches or leaves of trees or other plants which they thought would appease the god being worshiped. As recorded in Acts: "Then the priest of Jupiter, which was before their city, brought oxen and garlands unto the gates, and would have done sacrifice with the people. Which when the apostles, Barnabas and Paul, heard of, they rent their clothes, and ran in among the people, crying out, and saying, Sirs, why do you these things?" (Acts 14:13–15).

Earlier they witnessed Paul curing a cripple and said, ". . . the gods have come down to us in the likeness of men." They identified Paul with Mercury and Barnabas with Jupiter. Trying to pay them honor by placing garlands around their necks as gods, they were disappointed when the honor was repulsed. Yet, in a short time their adoration was changed to persecution in which Paul was stoned (Acts 14:19, 20).

In the early Olympic games, 348 B.C., the victors were presented a palm branch by the judges of the events. This was followed by the presentation of some item of value on the last day. However, this practice was stopped on command of the Delphic oracle and victors were subsequently graced by a wreath made from leaves of the sacred olive near Olympia which was said to have been planted by Neracles. This was deemed a sufficient reward.

The apostle Paul alludes to these sporting events in his epistles and refers to the wreath as a "corruptible crown" (1 Cor. 4:9; 9:24–27; 15:32; Phil. 3:14; Col. 3:15; 2 Tim. 2:5; 4:7, 8; Heb. 10:33; 12:1).

The Greek Olympic games were religious exercises dedicated to the Greek gods Zeus and Apollo. Since, beginning in 461 B.C., the participants performed naked, negative reaction to this practice was uncompromising by the Israelites.

In early Rome, an oak wreath was given as an award to a soldier who saved the life of a comrade in battle.

Garlands were used in birth feasts in 200 B.C. among the wealthy. Seven days after the birth of a child the house was decorated with garlands and olive branches, and friends and relatives were then invited to the event.

Incense

Incense is a substance that burns and emits a smell. From ancient biblical days to the present, it has been used in religious worship.

Incense does not come from a particular tree or plant, but is compounded from several substances of plant origin among which trees are prominent.

When the tabernacle was erected by Moses at the command of God, altars were constructed in it for two primary purposes. One was for the offering of sacrifices, the other for the burning of incense (Exod. 30:1).

The Sumerians built great temples to their gods. In these the priests and priestesses burned incense and offered daily sacrifices of animal and vegetable food.

Jeroboam, who stood before the altar to burn incense in

idolatrous worship, saw the altar "rent and ashes pour out." At this point his hand also "dried up so that he could not pull it in again" (1 Kings 13:2–5).

Upper classes in Egypt fumigated their homes with incense to ward off the foul odors of the crowded lower classes.

The Dead Sea Scrolls refer to the use of incense by those assigned to religious office during war time. They were "to attend to burnt-offerings and the sacrifices, to set out the incense of pleasant savor for God's acceptance."

Apparently incense prepared by the Hebrews was not desired by others. Herodotus reports on a merchant in Corinth who purchased a large quantity. He could not sell it since not a worshiper in Corinth would buy it.

Incense is still widely used today for religious purposes in many churches.

Manna

On the fifteenth day of the second month following their departure from Egypt, the Israelites came to the wilderness of Sin, between Elim and Sinai *(Fig. 3–10)*. At this location they complained bitterly to Moses and Aaron over the lack of food (Exod. 16:1, 2). As a consequence, God provided manna. "And when the dew that lay was gone up, behold, upon the face of the wilderness there lay a small round thing, as small as the hoar frost on the ground. And when the children of Israel saw it, they said one to another, it is manna: for they wist not what it was" (Exod. 16: 14, 15).

Manna means, "What is this?"

"And it was like coriander seed, white; and the taste of it was like wafers made with honey" (Exod. 16:31). Moses told the Israelites that this was the bread which the Lord gave them to eat.

Josephus described it "like honey in sweetness and pleasant taste but like in its body to bdellium, one of the sweet spices, and in brightness equal to coriander seed."

Was the manna of Moses' day the same as that which is collected today? Some scientists are of the belief that such is the case. Throughout the area traversed by Moses the tamarix tree, *Tamarix mannifera,* is indigenous. On this tree are found scale insects or lice. The insect species *Trabutina mannipara* is found mainly on tamarix in the mountain region, while *Najococcus serpentinus minor* is found on tamarix in the lowlands. In their feeding habits, these insects cause a tree to secrete a resinous sticky substance, which falls to the ground. It is said to fall about daybreak and it hangs in beads on the grass, twigs, and stones. Whitish in color at first, it subsequently turns to yellowish brown. It is sweet in taste and sticks to the teeth. Thus, it seems to resemble what Moses referred to as manna. It also has nutritional properties.

"And they gathered it every morning, every man according to his eating: and when the sun waxed hot it melted" (Exod. 16:21). Today, the Bedouins of the Sinai hasten to collect this substance in the early morning hours since ants are competitors and will eat all of the substance. Moses said that if the substance was left until the morning, "It bred worms and stank" (Exod. 16:20). Scientists believe the ants are the "worms" to which Moses had reference.

The Israelites ate manna for forty years, until they came to Canaan (Exod. 16:35).

In the Book of Revelation, manna is the symbol for immortality: "I will give him to eat of the hidden manna" (Rev. 2:17).

Today the substance described above is marketed commercially as Mannite. It is said an individual can collect up to four pounds a day in a good season. The substance must be sealed when collected.

It can be said that the manna collected today is, in a sense, the product of a tree. Is it, however, the manna of Moses' day? The provision of manna was a divine miracle sent to the Israelites in a time of need. Also, a double supply was given on Friday and not on the Sabbath (Josh.

5:12; Ps. 78:24). Did God, in his infinite wisdom, leave it for successive generations? Or, is this so-called manna another substance?

Josephus reported that manna was "falling down" in his day. "Even now, in all that place, this manna comes down in rain," he said.

"A golden pot that had manna" (Heb. 9:4) was among the contents of the ark of the covenant for a memorial. It was a tradition among the Jews that the ark, the tables of stone, the holy anointing oil, Aaron's rod, and the manna were hidden when Jerusalem was captured by the Chaldeans. Yet we know that when King Solomon placed the ark in the Temple, only the tables of stone were therein (1 Kings 8:9).

Medication

Use of the parts of trees, woody plants and herbs, or products therefrom, for medicinal purposes dates back to an early period in history. In every culture and in every age man has looked to plants to cure his diseases and relieve his physical suffering. While there has been a certain amount of mysticism and superstition attached to the healing power of trees and other plants, nature has provided many of them with substances containing medicinal qualities.

In ancient cultures the view prevailed that sickness was caused by demons which invaded the body. Diseases were thought to be signs of vengeance caused by superior beings. It was also thought that foul-tasting substances, combined with chants, prayers, and charms were needed to drive them out. The vile substance, it was assumed, would make the body an unpleasant place in which to live. Even today in China it is thought that illness is caused by "yin and yan life forces."

Records as early as 2500 B.C. in Bible lands list over 200 drugs and cultivated medicinal plants. Egyptian accounts of 1600 B.C. refer to the use of olive oil, pomegranate bark, elderberry, myrrh, cassia, and other plants for medicinal purposes. Ancient Hebrews, Babylonians, and Assyrians were very familiar with these drug plants.

Egyptians were noted for their medical knowledge (Jer. 46:11) and no doubt Moses acquired such knowledge during his sojourn in Egypt which he passed on to the Hebrews.

German Egyptologist George Ebers discovered a medical document of about 1550 B.C. known as the Ebers Papyrus. It contained extensive information on surgical practices and internal medicine and listed 800 medical drugs used in this period of history.

Sumerian tablets of about 200 B.C. indicate that the healing art was practiced in this nation as well. One prescription of this period suggested the pulverizing "of the dried vine, pine tree and plum tree; pour beer over it, rub with oil, fasten as poultice."

The Essenes, according to Josephus, "inquire after such roots and medical stones as may cure their distempers."

As early as 4000 B.C. in China many drugs from trees and other plants were used for medicinal purposes. Sanskrit writings describe the methods used to gather and prepare them for use.

For centuries high prices were paid for medicinal concoctions prepared by Arabs who controlled the spice and drug trade.

Primitive man determined the medical value of plants by trial and error, with perhaps dire consequences to some of those treated. It was the medicine man who had the main source of knowledge, and it was on the basis of such observations that early doctors were guided.

In 466 B.C., the father of medicine, Hippocrates, used cinnamon, acacia, and willow, to name a few plants, in his medical practice. He prescribed willow bark for fever and pain. Today we know that it is a source of salicylate, the principal ingredient of aspirin. Greeks were familiar with many present-day drug plants and the "root diggers" were an important caste in ancient Greece.

Following the Dark Ages the "Doctrine of Signatures" came to be accepted by many. Its thesis was that plant remedies could be identified by their resemblance to the afflicted organ, signs given by the Creator which indicated their intended use. Thus, a plant with a heart-shaped leaf would provide a substance good for the heart. Some common names of plants in use today come from this belief. Fortunately, this doctrine was not long-lived.

Man in biblical times suffered many diseases. Among those mentioned in the Bible are ague, boils and blains, consumption, dropsy, dysentery, emerods, epilepsy, fever, insanity, issue of blood, itch, leprosy, palsy, scab, sunstroke, ulcers, and worms. For these there were plant remedies in one form or another.

Perhaps the best known medication referred to in the Bible was the balm of Gilead used principally as an ointment for healing wounds (Jer. 46:11; 8:22). Another is the use of figs for boils (Isa. 38:21; 2 Kings 20:7). Ointment was used for "wounds, bruises and putrifying sores" (Isa. 1:6; James 5:14; Luke 10:34). The use of the leaves of plants for medicinal purposes was recognized (Ezek. 47:12), and wine was prescribed for its healing qualities (1 Tim. 5:23). Many other references to medicine are to be found throughout the pages of Scripture. Even psychiatry was touched upon in Proverbs 17:22 in which it is stated, "A merry heart doeth good like a medicine." It is repeated in Ecclesiastes 10:19. Yet, overuse of wine is condemned (1 Thess. 5:8).

It is known that fresh figs were rubbed upon the eyes of children to prevent opthalmia.

An interesting treatment pertaining to the health of horses was found in tablets in the ruins of the Phoenician seaport of Ugarit. The tablets, a veterinary guide for the period 1500 B.C., said, "If a horse has a sore nose, prepare a salve from figs and raisins, mixed with oatmeal and liquid. The mixture should be poured into the horse's nostrils."

Today we are still dependent upon drugs from the roots, bark, stems, flowers, seeds, and fruits of many plants, and the search is continuing. Quinine from the bark of the cinchona tree for the treatment of malaria, and oil from the chaulmooga tree in arresting the progress of leprosy are but two major contributions which woody plants have made to our health. Among the many other trees used today for medicinal purposes are wild cherry for cough syrup, witch hazel for lotion, and eucalyptus for nasal sprays.

Nuts

In Bible times nuts were a luxury food. Walnuts were universally cultivated and greatly esteemed. The nuts mentioned in the Song of Solomon (6:11) are believed to be walnuts.

The nuts of Genesis (43:11) are assumed to be pistachios, extensively eaten in Bible lands.

The Phoenicians grew walnuts as did the Greeks, Egyptians, and Chinese. Almond nuts and pine seed were also used as food.

Oil

Most references to oil in the Bible are to olive oil, although other animal and plant substances were known and used by the early people in Bible lands. The oil of myrrh is specifically mentioned in Esther 2:12. There was no petroleum oil used as we know it today.

Olive oil was a staple food and bread was dipped in it and eaten. It was also used as a cooking oil, in medication, for lighting, and for ritual and anointing purposes. Oil was a principal ingredient in making soap as well (Jer. 2:22). However, in Old Testament times their soap was not the type we use today. Then clothes, cooking utensils, and the body were cleaned with the ashes of certain alkali plants (Mal. 3:2).

Wounded animals were treated with olive oil for its soothing and curative effects (Ps. 23:5). It was used by the people as a cosmetic, to give hair a smooth appearance, and for a clean skin (Ps. 104:15).

As an anointing oil for ritual and religious purposes, the oil was usually combined with other ingredients (Exod. 30:22–25). Such was used to inaugurate men of rank into high office. Priests (Exod. 28:41; 29:7), prophets and kings (1 Kings 19:15, 16), and those who were "called" (Lev. 4:3, 5, 16; 1 Sam. 2:10; 1 Chron. 16:22) were among the ones so anointed.

Anointing the head of a guest with oil was considered, during the biblical period, as a mark of courtesy and is evident in the Twenty-third Psalm.

It is interesting to note that the Jews did not make use of oil prepared by foreigners.

Olive oil was the prime source of light in the tabernacle and in the dwellings of the people *(Fig. 19–1)*.

Olive oil is still widely used today for many purposes.

Fig. 19–1. A typical oil lamp used in the dwellings of the people prior to and during the time of Christ. Olive oil was placed in the vessel. A wick was placed in the spout. Though little known, olive oil exceeds all other plant oil in terms of brightness and steadiness of flame.

Ointments and Perfumes

Trees played an important role in providing the demands of man for the ointments and perfumes needed in religious worship and for personal use. Originally, it appears, these substances were used for ceremonial purposes. Eventually their use became a personal habit with an increasingly sophisticated society, and especially with the need for deodorants in hot lands where baths were infrequent (Esth. 2:12; Prov. 7:17; Isa. 57:9). They helped to cover bad smells and made life more enjoyable.

During the reign of Pharaoh Ramses, workers at a Theban graveyard went on strike because there were no ointments.

Ointments were used as cosmetics (Ruth 3:3) and considered precious (2 Kings 20:13). The smell of ointment was considered by Solomon as above that of spices (Song of Sol. 4:10). They were also used as hair oil (Eccl. 9:8) and for healing "wounds, bruises and putrifying sores" (Isa. 1:6), as well as nonsacred anointment. There were several grades of ointments, some being most costly (Amos 6:6).

Perfumes were generally in the form of ointments.

In early Egypt, those of financial means were literally drenched with perfumes and ointments by women servants. This usually happened following sumptuous feasts. Even the graves of the rich were stocked with decorated boxes containing ointment, flasks of perfume, and unguent spoons. One Egyptian text, found in an excavation, said: "Love thy wife at home as fitting. Fill her belly. Clothe her back. Ointment is the prescription for her body. Make her heart glad as long as thou liveth." Ladies of rank even wore sandals that emitted a perfume as they walked.

The practice of using perfumes and ointments became so widespread and universal that its disuse became an accepted sign of mourning (Deut. 28:40; Ruth 3:3; 2 Sam. 14:2; Dan. 10:3; Amos 6:6; Micah 6:15). Its use was considered as a courtesy to honored guests (Luke 7:46).

An interesting historical note is that reported by the Greek historian, Athenaeus. He states that the 400-foot funeral pyre of the Assyrian king of the ninth century B.C. was of perfumed wood and was kept burning for fifteen days.

The Bible contains many passages in which reference is made to a fondness for, and use of, perfumes. They were employed in religious rites (Exod. 30:7; 30:22–38; 35:28); in perfuming the garments and beds of those who could afford it (Prov. 7:17) and as a sign of courtesy to guests (Dan. 2:46); for application to the person (Prov. 27:9; Song of Sol. 3:6; Isa. 57:9); for embalming the dead (John 19:38–40); for burning with the dead (2 Chron. 16:14); and preparing a woman for marriage (Song of Sol. 1:12–14). Both the skin and hair were perfumed and anointed (Ps. 104:15) and on special occasions the scented unguent was used in profusion (Ps. 133:2).

In ancient Athens, when guests were invited to a feast, their beards were perfumed by censers of frankincense as they entered the house of their hosts. The hands were also scented after each lavation. Also, it was the custom to perfume the guests following the meal.

Many scents were used in compounding perfumes. That most frequently mentioned in the Bible is frankincense (Song of Sol. 3:6) and myrrh (Ps. 45:8). The process of compounding, however, is not known.

Moses refers to the religious perfume to be compounded from pure myrrh, sweet cinnamon, sweet calamus, cassia, and olive oil. A holy oil, made by a special formula, it could not be made or used by the Hebrews (Exod. 30). It was prepared by those who were apothecaries (Exod. 30:35; Eccl. 10:1).

Perfumes were sometimes kept in alabaster boxes or flasks (Luke 7:37). Such ointments were heavily scented and of high price (John 12:3, 5). They were manufactured chiefly from such ingredients as aloe, almug, cedar, bdellium, citrus, frankincense, myrrh, galbanum, saffron, onycha, stacte, cinnamon, spikenard, mardos, bitter almond, and cassia. These aromatics are thought to have used olive oil and perhaps fat as a base.

Aloe, thought to be derived from the "eagle tree" of India, and blended with myrrh and cinnamon, was used to perfume couches (Prov. 7:17) and to give fragrance to the robes of royalty (Ps. 45:8).

Bezaleel is the first perfume maker mentioned in the Bible. He prepared holy anointing oil and sacred incense (Exod. 37:29).

In spite of the achievements of modern science in developing synthetic scents, natural ingredients are still used today on a large scale.

Rope

For twine, string, and rope, early biblical people used flax and other materials. Fibers of the date palm tree were used extensively in making large ropes for general purposes. Many such palm ropes have been found in excavations of Upper and Lower Egypt. Fragments of such rope have also been found at Solomon's seaport of Ezion-geber. Some of these were made from twisted palm branches while the larger ones were made of hundreds of fibers taken from the palm bark. Evidently these ropes were used in connection with Solomon's fleet of ships.

There are many biblical references to rope; however, they do not give the source of the fibers used.

Rahab used a rope to let the spies over the wall of Jericho (Josh. 2:1–16); and Delilah bound Samson with a rope (Judg. 15:11, 12). Rope was also used in hangings for the court of the tabernacle (Num. 4:26). By a rope Paul was let down in a basket from an upper floor to escape the wrath of King Aretas (2 Cor. 11:33), while Jeremiah was lowered into an underground dungeon by a cord (Jer. 38:6, 13). Worn about the head, a rope was a symbol of deep servility (1 Kings 20:31, 32).

We do know that twine, string, and rope were used for many common purposes in the everyday life of the people in Bible days, just as they are today.

Spices

Spices are produced from various aromatic or pungent vegetative plants among which many trees are included. Usually we associate spices with such items as pepper, cinnamon, and ginger used in a powdered form to flavor food. Yet, the variety and usages of spices are many today, even as they were in Bible times.

The principal spices referred to by Moses that went into the holy anointing oil were myrrh, cinnamon, calamus, and cassia (Exod. 30:23, 24). They were mixed with oil to make them more durable and more easily applied (Exod. 30:25). Moses also had prepared a special perfume made from the spices stacte, onycha, galbanum, and frankincense (Exod. 30:34–36). This perfume played an important role in worship.

Spices were used to perfume garments. Psalm 45:8 refers to the use of myrrh, aloes, and cassia for this purpose. Beds were also perfumed with myrrh, aloes, and cinnamon (Prov. 7:17). King Asa was buried on a bed in a tomb "which was filled with sweet odors and divers kinds of spices—and they made a very great burning for him" (2 Chron. 16:14).

Spices were used in preparing the body of Jesus for burial. Nicodemus brought about 75 pounds of costly myrrh and aloes (John 19:19, 40) to the tomb for this purpose. This aloes is not the aloe of medicine, but rather it is from the highly scented wood of the *Aguilaria agallochum* tree. Nicodemus was a man of wealth and could afford the cost of these spices.

Spices were also brought to the tomb after Christ arose from the dead (Mark 16:1).

Joseph was taken to Egypt by a caravan of Midianites. At the time, they were carrying spices, balm, and myrrh, much in demand by Egyptians (Gen. 37:25).

Spices had various uses. They were burned as incense in the temples, used for embalming the bodies of nobility, as well as by the physicians in healing the sick.

In the early biblical period, caravans of spice merchants traveled from the Persian Gulf across Arabia to Petra, in the mountain fastness south of the Dead Sea. From here they traveled to Gaza and thence up the Mediterranean coast or along the east shore of the Dead Sea and along the Jordan River to Damascus. Many spices had their origin in India or Arabia.

In the ancient world, Arabia was the principal exporter of spices. Sheba, in Yemen, was one of four countries which, from available records, made up the Spice Kingdom whose capital was at Marib.

From historical records the country known as the Spice Kingdom was a garden of spices from the year 1500 to about 542 B.C. During this period a natural high dam across the river Adhanat *(Fig. 19–2)* provided water for irrigating

Fig. 19–2. Remains of the great dam at Marib in South Arabia. With its collapse in 542 B.C. fell an ancient commercial empire known throughout the civilized world for its frankincense and myrrh. The Queen of Sheba once ruled this wealthy empire and paid a visit to Solomon about 900 B.C. (photo courtesy Aramco World Magazine and photographer Thomas Sennett).

the spice trees and other plants. When the dam burst in 542 B.C., the desert crept over the land. Such an event was considered by the people as an act of divine judgment for turning against their god.

Marib is located at the southern tip of the Arabian peninsula, about 6000 feet up on the eastern mountain range that skirts the Red Sea.

It was from the Yemen of today that the Queen of Sheba began her journey to visit King Solomon.

Spices, many from trees, played an important role in all civilizations of antiquity, and were eagerly sought by all nations. Rich and poor alike used them. While they had little or no food value, they did add flavor and aroma to food, making eating a greater pleasure.

Spices were also employed in making beverages, served as preservatives, and used in medicines. In addition, the aroma of spices overcame the smell of bad food and bodily odors.

Josephus reports that 500 slaves were required to carry the spices used for the funeral service of Herod the Great.

Sweets

Sweets, produced from blending honey, dates, nuts, and gum arabic, were plentiful in early Egypt and perhaps were of better quality than some of our candy bars today. Interestingly, trees played a role in providing this food.

Honey was probably man's first sweetening ingredient and its flavor was early recognized as being dependent upon the source of nectar. Linden and citrus trees produced, along with other plants, honey of quality. Malta was called Melita by the Greeks in Paul's time since it produced so much honey.

Honey has long been recognized as an excellent food for man as it is almost pure sugar. It was found throughout Bible lands.

When a child cried in biblical times, a piece of sponge

dipped in honey was placed in his mouth. Apparently this served to quiet the child.

Our breakfast sweet rolls had their counterpart in ancient times. Honey and olive oil were mixed into the dough as it was being made into bread. It was eaten warm and generally served with sour wine or meat gravy (John 13:26; 21:13).

Fruit and honey cakes, in which nuts were sometimes included, were in demand for private functions. These cakes were used for funeral offerings as well.

The Pannag mentioned in Ezekiel 27:17 is considered by biblical authorities to be a variety of candy or sweetmeat.

John the Baptist's meat was locusts and wild honey (Matt. 3:4). Honey from wild bees was common in the woods in early days (1 Sam. 14:25). It has been speculated by some that the "locusts" which made up part of the diet of John the Baptist were carob tree pods. There is no agreement on this point, however.

Tannins

Trees and other woody plants, through the contribution of tannin, made possible the development of leather. While most plants contain some amount of tannin, few species contain a sufficient amount to be of economic importance.

Tannins are important in that they unite with certain types of proteins in animal skins to form the substance known as leather. Tannin is an astringent which causes tissue to constrict and is believed to cause the inactivity of certain enzymes.

An old art, tanning was known by Egyptians from whom the Israelites obtained such knowledge (Exod. 25:5). It was practiced by the Chinese over 3000 years ago. Even the Indians of our nation were knowledgeable about the tanning of buffalo hides.

The leather cutters of Egypt were considered so important that a part of the Libyan port of the city of Thebes was set aside for their industry. Among the items they made were thongs, sandals, shoes, coverings for the seats of sofas and chairs, chariot ornaments, shields, and harp adornments. Mention is made in the Bible of its use for tent coverings (Exod. 26:14) and water containers (Gen. 21:14). Milk (Judg. 4:19) and wine (Matt. 9:17) were also stored in leather. Certain types of shields were made of leather (2 Sam. 1:21; Isa. 21:5). Elijah and John the Baptist were wearers of leather garments which was a prophet's apparel (2 Kings 1:8; Matt. 3:4).

The tanner, a dresser of hides (Acts 9:43), was often ostracized in a community because of the odors created in the production of leather. As such, tanners lived outside the city, near a water source. Simon the tanner lived by the seashore at Joppa (Acts 10:6).

For the tannin in the biblical period, the bark of oak trees and the acrid juices of desert plants were used. Oak bark has been universally used throughout man's history, although the bark of other trees such as hemlock, mangrove, and wattle has been used in recent centuries. The woods of chestnut and quebracho were also a source of tannin in this later period, as were the leaves, fruits, and roots of certain plants.

It is interesting to note that early man knew oak galls had a high tannin content. Oak galls, formed on oaks, are the result of an insect which pierces the stem of a tree causing an abnormal growth.

Writing Inks

Inks of one form or another have been used since the dawn of civilization. As early as 2500 B.C., Egyptians were using ink on papyrus. Red was made from red ochre. A carbon ink, the most common, was a combination of charcoal, gum arabic, and water. At times varnish was used as a substitute for water. The charcoal was produced from date fruit stones, vegetable soot, or was of animal origin. The ink was intensely black and would retain its color for ages, yet was easily removed from parchments with sponge and water.

Later, tannin was employed in combination with iron salts for use in writing inks. As recorded in the eleventh century, tannin was obtained from the insect galls taken from the Aleppo oak, *Quercus infectoria*. Such galls have a high tannic content. Sulphate of iron was mixed with the galls and gum. The material was pulverized and moistened with water when used as an ink.

According to Josephus, both the Egyptians and Hebrews made use of different colors for writing, with red, purple, blue, gold, and silver tints.

Ink used by the early Hebrew copyists of the Scriptures was strictly regulated by the Talmud. Only black ink of the purest kind could be used. It consisted of charcoal soot and honey mixed together to form a paste. This was allowed to harden. Before being used, this paste was dissolved in water, with an "infusion of galls."

Of religious interest is that the copyist was not to dip his pen into the ink immediately before writing the sacred name. Rather, he had to do so when transcribing the preceding word.

Ink is mentioned only once in the Old Testament, where Baruch says he wrote Jeremiah's prophecies "with ink" (Jer. 36:18). It occurs just three times in the New Testament (2 Cor. 3:3; 2 John 12; 3 John 13).

Writing Materials

Ancient writing materials included clay, wax, metal, plaster, and wood (Deut. 27:2, 3; Josh. 8:32; Luke 1:63). Later, parchment and papyrus were used (2 Tim. 4:13; 2 John 12).

The bark of trees was used as a writing material in Rome until replaced by papyrus late in the second century B.C.

However, to a limited extent, bark was so utilized up to the fifth century A.D.

Excavated records from the period 700 B.C. show that slabs of wood, coated with stucco, were used in Mesopotamia for writing purposes. Some of these slabs were hinged.

In 200 B.C., students were first taught to write on a wooden board having its sides covered with wax. The writer used a wooden stylus, pointed at one end to inscribe characters on the wax. The other end of the stylus was used to rub out mistakes or bad penmanship. When the student became proficient he advanced to a roll of Nile papyrus.

It was Ancus Marcius, in ancient Rome, who published the religious ceremonies on whited boards and hung them up around the forum for all to see and observe. This was done under the command of King Numa. During the time of Flavius, whited boards were still used in the forum, but served for informational purposes.

The pen which used ink was made from the hollow stem of a plant, usually a rush. It was cut diagonally with a knife to form a flexible point. To keep the pen in good writing order, the scribe had to re-cut the stem with the knife. This is the origin of the term "pen knife" (Jer. 36:23).

In the New Testament it is said that Moses was "educated in all the wisdom of the Egyptians" (Acts 7:22). No doubt Moses was an expert in writing Egyptian hieroglyphics. The discovery of the Tel el-Amarna tablets indicates how extensive was the knowledge and use of writing during his lifetime. In Egypt, writing was done principally on papyrus and dates back to about 2800 B.C.

A stylus, made from metal or wood, was used for writing on hard material (Exod. 32:4).

The inkhorn, carried in the girdle by scribes, held the pens and ink. These were made from metal or wood.

It is speculated that the sign placed on the cross above Christ (Luke 28:33; John 19:19) was written by Pilate on a whitened board with black letters.

20

Memorable Trees of the Bible

THERE ARE A NUMBER of so-called memorable trees (*Fig. 20–1*) in the Bible. These are trees to which special reference is made by Bible writers. They are associated with some special event. They were accorded special attention by the people. Some of the most notable are the following:

Allon-bachuth Oak

When Jacob and his wife Rebekah were at Bethel, Deborah, Rebekah's old nurse, died. She was buried beneath an oak tree in the valley below Bethel, "And the name of it was called Allon-bachuth," the Oak of Weeping (Gen. 35:8).

Oak of Gibeah

It was under this oak that Saul sat, "having his spear in hand, and all his servants were standing about him," when

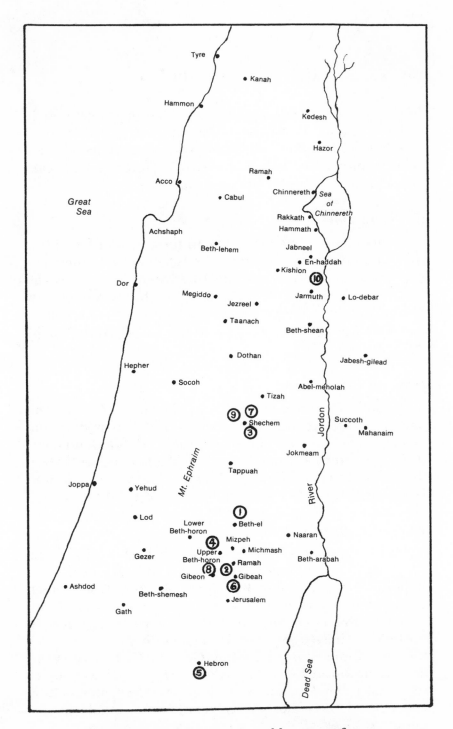

Fig. 20–1. Map showing general locations of some memorable trees of the Bible. *Key:* 1) Allon-bachuth Oak, 2) Oak of Gibeah, 3) Covenant Oak, 4) Deborah's Palm Tree, 5) Trees of Ephron, 6) Migron Pomegranate, 7) Diviner's Oak, 8) Oak of Tabor, 9) Oak of the Pillar, and 10) Oak in Zaanannim.)

he accused his officers and his son of being against him, in favor of David. It was near this point where he had 85 priests killed (1 Sam. 22:6–18). The King James Version refers to only a tree in Ramah without reference to species. Others refer to it as an oak or tamarisk.

Covenant Oak

Joshua made a covenant with all the tribes of Israel that they would not worship strange gods, committing them to a permanent and binding contract between themselves and God. "And Joshua wrote these words in the book of the law of God, and took a great stone, and set it up there under an oak, that was by the sanctuary of the Lord" (Josh. 24:23–26).

Deborah's Palm Tree

Deborah, the wife of Lapidoth, was a prophetess who judged Israel. It was her responsibility to restore the people to the worship of the one true God. She held court under a palm tree located between Ramah and Bethel, in the hill country of Mount Ephraim. "And the children of Israel came up to her for judgment" (Judg. 4:4, 5).

Trees of Ephron

Sarah, Abraham's wife, died at the age of 127 years. Abraham mourned and wept over his loss. He purchased from Ephron, at a cost of 400 pieces of silver, land "which was in Machpelah, which was before Mamre, the field, and the cave which was therein, and all the trees that were in the field." These trees were Abraham's "beloved trees." In the cave Abraham buried Sarah (Gen. 23:17–19). The trees are also referred to as the Oaks of Mamre. It was under these oaks that Abraham saw three travelers approaching and offered them hospitality. They were angels in disguise.

Migron Pomegranate

"And Saul tarried in the uttermost part of Gibeah under a pomegranate tree which is in Migron: and the people that were with him were about six hundred men." While he tarried, his son Jonathan and his armorbearer, unknown to him, delivered Israel from its enemies (1 Sam. 14:2–23).

Diviner's Oak

Diviner's oak, otherwise known as the "Oak of Meonenim," is referred to in the Revised Standard Version. It is translated "plain" in the King James Version but most biblical authorities consider this a mistranslation. It is usually translated "oak" (Judg. 9:37).

The diviner's oak was a tree near Shechem, along a road or trail upon which people traveled to the city. One writer suggests that it was probably a sacred tree where divination was practiced.

Oak of Tabor

Samuel said to Saul, "And when you get to the oak of Tabor you will see three men coming toward you who are on their way to worship God at the altar at Bethel." This was Samuel's second sign confirming the mission of Saul (1 Sam. 10:3 LB). The King James Version refers to the "plain of Tabor" which Bible authorities say should be "Oak of Tabor." The location of this tree is unknown today.

Oak of the Pillar

This was a sacred tree at a shrine in Shechem. It is also called the oak of Moreh. Under it Abimelech was made King of Israel, "by the oak of the pillar at Shechem" (Judg. 9:6 RSV). It has been suggested that this may have been the tree under which Jacob hid the gods and jewelry of his wives (Gen. 35:4) and under which Joshua set up a great stone house as a witness to the dedication of the people to the law of the Lord (Josh. 24:26).

There is a tradition that upon the conquest of the hill country of Mt. Gerizim, Mt. Ephraim, and Mt. Ebal, the Israelite sanctuary at the oaks of Moreh near Shechem (Gen. 12:4) became the central meeting area for the various tribes. For a long period there were Hebrew tribes near Shechem and thus the importance of the area at the start of the period of settlement of the Promised Land.

Oak in Zaanannim

It was to the family of Heber that Sisera the Canaanite fled, after his defeat by the Israelites, to Elon (oak of) Zaanannim, on the border between Naphtali and Issachar (Josh. 19:33; Judg. 4:11). It was evidently a holy site. Sisera sought refuge with this family, but Jael, Heber's wife, acted according to her conscience and killed him (Judg. 4:21).

Aside from its symbolism as a tree of strength, the oak of biblical lands also seems to have been connected with tragedy and sorrow.

21

✤ Tree
Superstitions

ARE YOU SUPERSTITIOUS ABOUT TREES? On occasion do you find yourself "knocking on wood"? Such a practice is common in our country. It's a practice that came from the medieval Druids of England and the Gauls, growing out of their worship of the oak and the mistletoe which grew upon it. To appease the spirits they tapped the tree gently. The parasitic mistletoe (*Fig. 21–1*) was considered of divine origin, symbolic of forked lightning. These rites were conducted within groves of trees.

In ancient Scandinavia, according to legend, enemies meeting by chance beneath a tree upon which mistletoe grew were obligated to disarm, embrace one another in friendship, and maintain peace for the balance of the day. It is speculated that from this legend came the custom of kissing beneath the mistletoe.

Many people of the world still hold to various supersti-

Fig. 21–1. Parasitic mistletoe was considered by the Druids and Gauls as being of divine origin. It entered into their worship of the gods. TFS

tions and myths about trees that had their origin among the heathen.

From ancient times trees have exerted a profound spiritual influence upon man. At first, as he wandered the land seeking the necessities of life, he lacked knowledge of his environment. As he entered a forest or went under a large tree, he no doubt beheld it in awe, such as one does upon entering a redwood forest today for the first time. And should he have been present in a forest when lightning struck a nearby tree, it would have been an emotional experience and one to bring on fear. The forest was also a place of animals which he may have feared (Mic. 5:8; Jer. 5:6).

A tree played a role in the dream of King Nebuchadnezzar who called before him the magicians, enchanters, Chaldeans, and astrologers to interpret it. This staff, available to the King, suggests that he was strongly superstitious. As the Bible records, only Daniel was able to interpret the dream (Dan. 4:4–27).

Litz, a Chinese philosopher of 450 B.C., refers to "islands in the easter ocean with trees whose fruit confer immortality."

The biblical attitude toward superstitions, idols, and divination was distinctly hostile (Deut. 18:10–12). There was but one true God. Yet, the Hebrews consistently turned to other gods and superstitions of the period. While a tattoo upon one's person was forbidden (Lev. 19:28), some branded their flesh with the deity they worshiped, such as the ivy leaf of Bacchus (3 Macc. 2:29).

Household gods of the Semitic nations are often mentioned in the Old Testament from the time of Laban (Gen. 31:19). These were wooden images (1 Sam. 19:13) consulted as idols. From these the excited worshipers assumed that they received oracular response (Ezek. 21:21; Zech. 10:2).

Hosea refers to divination by wooden rods. It is said that this was an invention of the Chaldeans. As practiced, two rods were held upright. They were allowed to fall while some form of incantation was uttered. The oracle which followed was based on the way in which the rods fell, whether forward or backward, or to the right or left. Said Hosea: "and their staff declareth unto them" (Hos. 4:12).

Superstitious Jews at the time of Christ wore "prayer fillets" on their left arms and between their eyes during prayer (Matt. 23:5). These were generally small wooden boxes in which were enclosed the scripture wording of Deuteronomy 11:13–22; 6:4–9; Exodus 13:11–16 and 13:1–10. The wearing of these "fillets" was prompted by a literal interpretation of Exodus 13:9, 16 which states: "And it shall be to you as a sign on your hand and as a memorial between your eyes. . . . It shall be as a mark on your hand or frontlets between your eyes."

Jeremiah relates how the people turned to the queen of heaven. Said he: "The children gather wood, the fathers kindle the fire, and the women knead their dough, to make cakes to the queen of heaven" (Jer. 7:18).

The ship in which Paul sailed from Malta bore the sign of Castor and Pollux (Acts 28:11). These were the ancient

Fig. 21–2. Does this large gnarled tree evoke any veneration from you? It does present a mystic appearance, and to the heathens it became an object of worship. They believed that such trees contained spirits with special powers. Gifts of food were often hung from the branches of such trees as offerings to the deities within. TFS

symbols of the heathen gods at Lacedaemon. They were represented on the ship by two parallel beams of wood, joined by crosspieces. Spartans took these symbols with them into war. As gods of the sea, they were worshiped particularly in Ostia.

Large spreading trees that were twisted and gnarled were especially venerated *(Fig. 21–2)*. To those who worshiped them, presumably they had special powers.

Lacking knowledge of his universe and the role that trees play, man became superstitious concerning trees. These superstitions led to myths and eventually to legends that have been passed down through succeeding generations to ours.

Heathen worship of trees and plants, in addition to wooden idols, existed during the time of the prophets, and the Bible has many references to such. Gifts of food were often hung on the branches of trees as offerings or sacrifices to the deities the heathen worshiped.

Trees were also venerated by heathen people who believed gods inhabited them (Deut. 12:2; 1 Kings 14:23). For this reason Hebrews were forbidden to plant a tree near a sacred altar (Deut. 16:21).

Since the prophets were unsuccessful in stamping out heathen practices, such beliefs spread to other people and continue to this day in one form or another in superstitions, myths or legends.

Ancient Egyptians, in celebrating the winter soltice, the shortest day of the year, brought green date palm leaves into their homes. To them, this was a symbol of "life triumphant over death," just as the sun starts its annual "triumph over darkness," or "rebirth" at this period. Likewise, to celebrate the return or "rebirth" of the sun, the Romans included in their feast of Saturn ceremony the raising of an evergreen bough. A festive occasion followed. The feast of Saturn was replaced by Christmas on December 25 in A.D. 354 after Christianity became the accepted religion in the Roman Empire.

Herodotus reported that Hebrew exorcists ejected demons from the human body by the smell of the smoke of a burning baaras plant. The power of curing epilepsy was also attributed to this plant.

Josephus says conjuration and exorcism were among the "wisdoms" of Solomon. He stated that Solomon had a skill to expel demons and compose incantations "by which distempers are alleviated." For this purpose a tree was involved.

To illustrate his point Josephus said that he saw a man named Eleazar perform, in view of others, the rite on a man possessed of the demon. "He put a ring that had a root of one of these sorts mentioned by Solomon to the nostrils of the demoniac, after which he drew out the demon through his nostrils; and when the man fell down immediately, he abjured him to return into him no more, making still mention of Solomon, and reciting the incantations which he composed. And when Eleazar would persuade and demonstrate to the spectators that he had such a power, he set a little off a cup or basin full of water, and commanded the demon, as he went out of the man, to overturn it and thereby to let the spectators know that he had left the man; and when this was done, the skill and wisdom of Solomon was shown manifestly."

The "root" to which Josephus refers was further described by him as coming from a "rue tree." Said he, "There is a certain place called Baaras which produces a root of the same name with itself; its color is like to that of flame and toward the evenings it sends out a certain ray of lightning. It is only valuable on account of one virtue it hath, that if it be brought to a sick person, it quickly drives away those called demons, which are no other than the spirits of the wicked, that enter into men that are alive and kill them, unless they can obtain some help against them."

Apparently this was the type of "black magic" practiced during the time of Paul (Acts 19:13–19), being derived from the idolatry and superstitions of heathen worshipers. It may have been encouraged by Solomon in his old age when, because of his heathen wives, he had forsaken God, and God had forsaken him, and had given him up to demoniacal delusions (1 Kings 11:4–11).

To the Egyptians the fig was held sacred to the various deities, and especially to Hathor, the goddess of love. Its fruit and branches were placed as funerary offerings in the tombs of kings and noblemen.

The early Scandinavians are said to have offered homage to the fir tree. After they became Christians, they made evergreen trees part of their Christian festivals.

To the Druids of ancient Gaul, sprigs of evergreen brought into the home meant eternal life, while to the Norsemen such sprigs symbolized the revival of the god Balder. Superstitious individuals of these lands long believed that branches of evergreens placed over their doors would keep out ghosts, witches, and all forms of evil spirits.

It is reported that the Druids removed branches from a selected tree so that what branches were left formed a tau cross. This tree they preserved and venerated. At the base of this tree the Druids inscribed the word "Thau," by which they meant "god." On the right branch of the limb forming the cross, they inscribed the word "Hesuls," and on the left branch the word "Belen" or "Belenus." In the middle they inscribed "Tharamis." This represented a sacred triad. Its significance is unknown.

Nymphs were known and celebrated wherever Hellenic culture spread. They were believed to inhabit desolate places such as forests, caves, streams, and unexplored land. Those inhabiting forests and trees were called dryads and were thought to be born with a tree and decay along with it. Shrines were dedicated to nymphs and offerings were made to them, including olive oil. Though the Grecians gave the greatest emphasis to them, they appeared in Roman mythology.

Romans used a tapered block of granite, with stylized trees carved on its sides, as a woodland divinity to protect the trees and boundaries of forests.

While the Romans did not have the rich mythology of the Greeks, they did bow down and worship rocks and wood. A wooden gate in the Roman Forum was worshiped as a god. This was the two-headed Janua (January), the god of gates who could look forward and backward at the same time.

Oak appears to have been especially venerated in heathen worship and it was considered the noblest expression of vegetable life. The Oracle of Zeus at Dodona was an oak tree in Greek mythology. Even oak galls, caused by insects, were the objects of superstition centuries ago. The oak was also held sacred by the Greeks, Romans, Teutons, and Celts. Thor, the "Thunder God," was believed to love the oak since he caressed it with his lightning. It was a

Celtic practice to burn a Yule oak log to influence Yaioul, the god of fire, to bring a moderate winter season. Today, some carry an acorn in their pockets to be blessed with perpetual youth.

Juniper, more commonly called cedar in our nation, is considered by some people today as an omen of death and under no condition would they transplant such a tree. If they did, it would presumably bring an untimely death to the planter or a member of the family. Even young volunteer trees in a yard are cut down quickly to avoid serious consequences. Some hold to the belief that if a small cedar is transplanted the planter will die when the tree becomes large enough to shade a grave.

Some Canadian lumbermen will not sleep in a logging camp built from aspen logs. They believe that the aspen has been trembling since the crucifixion of Christ.

When a maiden places an apple beneath her pillow and prays for a glimpse of her future husband she is merely continuing a veneration bestowed long ago upon the "sacred fruit" by Aphrodite.

In Sweden today there is an ancient legend of a tree with power to cure sickness in children. Even in our modern society there are those who "communicate" with certain trees to which they have an "affinity."

Many superstitions and myths about trees or products of trees exist today. They range from a cure for asthma to providing perpetual youth, and have their origins in heathen worship of biblical times.

A few of the many common myths about trees are the following: to kill an unwanted tree, cut a hickory stick and lean it against the tree to be deadened; a splint from a tree struck by lightning can stop a toothache, if the splinter is used to pick the offending tooth; it is bad luck to accept a cedar tree as a gift without giving something in return;

planting a willow tree will bring either a death in the family or other bad luck; and it is good luck to carry a buckeye in a pocket.

The Maypole dance had its origin in a heathen Attis ceremony to the spirits which lived in the forest. It was believed such acts would insure fertility in man and animals. Presumably the dance around the tree or pole was symbolic of the Tree of Life.

Consciously or subconsciously, man has a close relationship to trees.

22 🍁🍁🍁🍁🍁🍁🍁🍁🍁🍁🍁🍁🍁🍁

🍁 The Crown of Thorns and the Burning Bush

The Crown of Thorns

"And when they had platted a crown of thorns, they put it upon his head" (Matt. 27:29). Such were the words Matthew used to describe the crown made from some thorny plant and placed upon Christ's head in mockery.

While the crown's primary purpose was not to cause suffering, which it must have done, its principal purpose was to excite ridicule. In that period of history, as today, crowns designated honor and were worn only by priests, kings, and queens (Exod. 28:36–38; 2 Chron. 23:11; Esth. 2:17). But the soldiers put the crown on Jesus' head "... and mocked him, saying, Hail, King of the Jews!" (Matt. 27:29).

The species of plant from which the crown was made is unknown. It may have been the plant *Calcotome illosa*

Fig. 22–1. Pictured here is what is commonly called Christ's thorn tree located near Rafiach in north Sinai near the coast. It is estimated to be 150 years old and is unusually large for this species. Note effect of wind erosion on the roots which lie exposed about two feet above present surface of the ground. It is presumed by some that Christ's crown of thorns came from a tree of this kind. SL

which grows near Jerusalem. The Crusaders thought it to be *Zizyphus spina-Christi,* or palinrus shrub *(Fig. 22–1),* which grows in Judaea and is known as Syrian Christ's thorn. A tree which generally ranges in height from ten to fifteen feet, it is easily recognized by its whitish twigs and yellowish-green flowers.

The original "Crown of Thorns" is claimed by the Golden Cathedral on the island of Palma. The cathedral, dating from 1230, contains the tombs of two of Mallorca's four kings and that of the anti-Pope Clement VII who died in 1447. There is no scientific proof as to the claim made for the crown held there.

The Burning Bush

Moses was astonished to see a woody plant on fire that was not consumed, this was one of the many miracles performed by the Lord. As told in the biblical account: "And the angel of the Lord appeared to him in a flame of fire out of the midst of a bush: and he looked, and, behold, the bush burned with fire, and the bush was not consumed" (Exod. 3:2).

The species of plant involved in this event is unknown. There is speculation, however, that it may have been one of the many thorny green plants indigenous at this period of history to the Sinai. It has been suggested that the bush may have been an acacia, *Acacia tortilis,* or *Zizyphus spina Christi.* However, one of many other plants may have been used by the Lord for his purpose.

The Parable
of the Trees
and
Its Message to All Ages

IT IS APPROPRIATE in this last chapter to close with a parable of trees that has as much application today as when it was first pronounced centuries ago. It is called the "Parable of the Trees" as recorded in Judges 9.

The parable told by Jotham, son of Gideon, dealt with three of the most beloved and useful plants of the Bible, namely the olive tree, the fig tree, and the vine *(Fig. 23–1)*.

Said Jotham in his pronouncement: "The trees went forth, on a time, to anoint a king over them: and they said to the olive tree, Reign thou over us. But the olive tree said unto them, Should I leave my fatness, wherewith by me they honor God and man, and go to be promoted over the trees? And the trees said to the fig tree, Come thou, and reign over us. But the fig tree said unto them, Should I forsake my sweetness, and my good fruit, and go to be promoted over the trees? Then said the trees unto the vine,

Fig. 23–1. "And the vine said unto them, Should I leave my wine, which cheereth God and man, and go to be promoted over the trees?" (Judges 9:13). Shown is a grape vine growing in a wild state on an area planted to trees. Grape is one of the most beloved and useful plants of the Bible. CGI

Come thou, and reign over us. And the vine said unto them, Should I leave my wine, which cheereth God and man, and go to be promoted over the trees? Then said all trees unto the bramble, Come thou, and reign over us. And the bramble said unto the trees, If in truth ye anoint me king over you, then come and put your trust in my shadow: and if not, let fire come out of the bramble, and devour the cedars of Lebanon" (Judg. 9:8–15).

Following the death of Gideon, a man of God, there was no spiritual and political leader who was willing to assume his place at that moment. Moral decay set in. God was forgotten. The people were ungrateful to God for the favors he had bestowed upon them as a nation.

A potential tyrant surfaced under these conditions. His name was Abimelech, son of Gideon by his concubine. He had a lust for power, and he quietly and effectively carried on a campaign that appealed to the people but lacked integrity. He failed to heed the admonition of his father who said earlier to the people "I will not rule over you, neither shall my son rule over you: the Lord shall rule over you" (Judg. 8:23).

When he had sufficient and absolute power, Abimelech murdered all the sons of Gideon except Jotham, the youngest, who escaped. With such power "all the men of Shechem gathered together, and all the house of Millo, and went, and made Abimelech king" (Judg. 9:6). It was then too late for the people to oppose him. They had made a choice of an ungodly man who had no real interest in their welfare.

Jotham, in his parable, referred to the olive tree, fig tree, and vine as representing those in society whose "fruits" and "works" are a blessing to mankind. They are people with integrity, and endowed with ability, experience, and training. Also, they are honest men of stature.

As pointed out by Jotham, each one refused to assume responsibilities of leadership. They were qualified and competent to take on the task of giving leadership, but were unwilling to sacrifice, as Gideon, their own self-interests for the welfare of all. Each was materialistic and self-centered. They were, they thought, good, godly men, but were unwilling to shoulder their civic responsibility. As individuals, they were not grateful for the heritage of freedom which was theirs, until it was too late.

It is only when good people are indifferent in any nation that injustice can prevail in any society. When they neglect their civic responsibilities, then the unworthy rise to power to the destruction of all that the people hold dear.

In closing this book the reader is reminded of the discussion that launched it. In the Genesis account of creation we are told that God, after creating plants, saw that they were good. Truly, trees and other woody plants have played an important role in the history of mankind as reflected through the pages of the Bible. Today they occupy an increasingly important position in the life of all people on the face of the earth. Indeed, our very survival could well depend upon our attitude toward this "good" creation of our God.

Yes, trees and woody plants are good!

Appendix

There are hundreds of references to trees and other woody plants in the Bible. A partial list of these follows:

Every good tree bringeth forth good fruit; but a corrupt tree bringeth forth evil fruit (Matt. 7:17).

For the tree is known by his fruit (Matt. 12:33).

Ye shall know them by their fruits . . . (Matt. 7:16).

And the leaves of the tree were for the healing of the nations (Rev. 22:2).

As the days of a tree are the days of my people (Isa. 65:22).

When thou shalt hear a sound of going in the tops of the mulberry trees, that then thou shalt go out to battle (1 Chron. 14:15).

To him that overcometh will I give to eat of the tree of life (Rev. 2:7).

The sound of a shaken leaf shall chase them (Lev. 26:36).

The trees went forth one at a time to anoint a king over them (Judg. 9:8).

The birds of the air come and lodge in the branches thereof (Matt. 13:32).

273

Hurt not . . . the trees (Rev. 7:3).

For he shall be as a tree planted by the waters . . . (Jer. 17:8).

The fig tree putteth forth her green figs (Song of Sol. 2:13).

I made me gardens and orchards, and I planted trees in them (Eccl. 2:5).

Behold, I am a dry tree (Isa. 56:3).

Every plant which my heavenly Father hath not planted, shall be rooted up (Matt. 15:13).

Then shall all the trees of the wood rejoice (Ps. 96:12).

And Solomon's wisdom excelled—and he spake of trees (1 Kings 4:30, 33).

For there is hope of a tree, if it be cut down, that it will sprout again, and that the tender branch thereof will not cease (Job 14:7).

Blessed are they that do his commandments, that they may have right to the tree of life . . . (Rev. 22:14).

I have made him fair by the multitude of his branches: so that all the trees of Eden, that were in the garden of God, envied him (Ezek. 31:9).

Who his own self bare our sins in his own body on the tree (1 Peter 2:24).

These are the two olive trees, and the two candlesticks standing before the God of the earth (Rev. 11:4).

And Judah and Israel dwelt safely, every man under his vine and under his fig tree (1 Kings 4:25).

Trees whose fruit withereth, without fruit, twice dead, plucked up by the roots (Jude 12).

Whose height was like the height of the cedars, and he was strong as the oaks (Amos 2:9).

All thy trees and fruit of thy land shall the locust consume (Deut. 28:42).

And he stood among myrtle trees (Zech. 1:8).

They are upright as the palm tree (Jer. 10:5).

For they shall be ashamed of the oaks (Isa. 1:29).

He moveth his tail like a cedar (Job 40:17).

And Jacob took him rods of green poplar, and of the hazel and chestnut tree (Gen. 30:37).

The beams of our house are cedar, and our rafters of fir (Song of Sol. 1:17).

A word fitly spoken is like apples of gold in pictures of silver (Prov. 25:11).

He lieth under the shady tree, in the covert of the reed (Job 40:21).

The fruit of all manner of trees . . . (Neh. 10:37).

The cedars in the garden of God could not hide him (Ezek. 31:8).

Then said all the trees unto the bramble, come thou, and reign over us. And the bramble said unto the tree, if in truth ye anoint me king over you, then come and put your trust in my shadow, and if not, let fire come out of the bramble, and devour the cedars of Lebanon (Judg. 9:14, 15).

Do men gather . . . figs of thistle? (Matt. 7:16).

He shall . . . cast off his flower as the olive (Job 15:33).

Thy children like olive plants round about thy table (Ps. 128:3).

A good tree cannot bring forth evil fruit, neither can a corrupt tree bring forth good fruit (Matt. 7:18).

And he made boards for the tabernacle of shittim wood, standing up (Exod. 36:20).

As the apple tree among the trees of the wood, so is my beloved among the sons . . . (Song of Sol. 2:3).

Bibliography

Abeles, Frederick. *Ethylene in Plant Biology.* Academic Press, 1973.

Aharoni, Yohanan, and Avi-Yonah, Michael. *The MacMillan Bible Atlas.* New York: The MacMillan Company, 1968.

American Archaeological Institute of America. *American Journal of Archaeology.*

American Spice Trade Association, Inc. *A History of Spices.* New York, 1960.

———. *Spices, What They Are—Where They Come From.* New York, 1959.

Balsiger, Dave, and Sellier, Charles, Jr. *In Search of Noah's Ark.* Los Angeles: Sun Classic Books, 1976.

Blaiklock, E. M. *The Zondervan Pictorial Bible Atlas.* Grand Rapids: Zondervan Publishing House, 1974.

Brothwell, Don, and Sandison, A. T. *Diseases of Antiquity.* Springfield, Illinois: Charles C. Thomas, 1967.

Bryan, Cyril P. *Ancient Egyptian Medicine, The Papyrus Ebers* (translation from the German version). Chicago: Ares Publishers, Inc., 1974.

Bryant, T. Alton. *The New Bible Dictionary.* Grand Rapids: Zondervan Publishing House, 1967.

Buttrick, George Arthur. *Interpreters Dictionary of the Bible.* New York: Abingdon Press, 1962.

Central Intelligence Agency. *Atlas Issues in the Middle East.* Washington, D.C.: U.S. Government Printing Office, 1973.

Clarke, Adam. *Commentary on the Holy Bible.* Grand Rapids: Baker Book House, 1967.

DeWitt, Karen. "All the Perfumes of Arabia." *Aramco World Magazine*, September-October, 1974.

Douglas, J. D. *The New Bible Dictionary*. Grand Rapids: Wm. B. Eerdmans Publishing Co., 1970.

Eckholm, Erik P. *The Other Energy Crisis: Firewood*. Washington, D.C.: Worldwatch Institute, 1975.

European Space Research Organization (EROS) Data Center. Aerial photographs of the Holy Lands, Sioux Falls.

Gali, L. *An Ancient Technique for Ripening Sycomore Fruit in East-Mediterranean Countries*. Economic Botany. Vol. 22, No. 2. April/June, 1968.

Gaster, Theodore H. *The Dead Sea Scriptures*. New York: Doubleday and Co., 1970.

————. *Myth, Legend, and Custom in the Old Testament*. New York: Harper and Row, 1969.

Gillespie, Charles Coulston. *Genesis and Geology*. Harvard University Press, 1951.

Grieve, Maud. *A Modern Herbal*. New York: Hafner Publishing Co., 1959.

Halley, Henry H. *Halley's Bible Handbook*. Minneapolis: Grason Company, 1962.

Hareuven, Nogah, and Frenkley, Helen. *Ecology in the Bible*. Neot Kedumim, Ltd., Kiryat Ono, Israel, 1974.

Hastings, James. *A Dictionary of the Bible*. New York: Charles Scribner's Sons, 1900.

Hill, Albert F. *Economic Botany*. New York: McGraw-Hill Book Co., 1968.

Hsu, Kenneth J. "When the Mediterranean Dried Up." *Scientific American*, December, 1972.

Iseminger, Gordon L. "Environmental Abuse and Neglect: Precursors of Civilization's Doom?" *N.D.Q. Quarterly*. The University of North Dakota, 1969.

James, E. O. *The Tree of Life*. Leiden, Netherlands: E. J. Brill, 1966.

Keller, Werner. *The Bible As History*. New York: William Morrow and Co., 1956.

Ketchum, Richard M. *The Secret Life of the Forest*. New York: American Heritage Press, 1970.

Lewis, G. Walton. *The House Which King Solomon Built for Jehovah*. Cincinnati: Standard Publishing Co., 1927.

Lindsell, Harold. *God's Incomparable Word*. Minneapolis. World Wide Publications, 1977.

Liphschitz, Nili and Waisel, Yoar. *The Effects of Human Activity on Composition of the Natural Vegetation During Historic Periods*. Israel: Tel-Aviv University. Undated.

––––––. *Analysis of the Botanical Material of the 1969–1970 Seasons and the Climatic History of Beer-Sheba Region*. Israel: Tel-Aviv University. Undated.

––––––. *Dendroarchaeological Investigations in Israel*. Israel: Tel-Aviv University, Undated.

Lowdermilk, W. C. *Conquest of the Land Through 7000 Years*. Agriculture Information Bulletin No. 99. Washington, D.C.: U.S. Dept. of Agriculture, 1953.

Matthews, Samuel W. "What's Happening to Our Climate." *National Geographic*, Washington, D.C.: National Geographic Society, November, 1976.

Mickey, Karl B. *Man and the Soil*. Chicago: International Harvester Co., 1945.

Miller, Hugh. *Testimony of the Rocks*. Boston: Gould and Lincoln, 1868.

Miller, Madeleine S. and Miller, J. Lane. *Encyclopedia of Bible Life*. Second Edition. New York: Harper and Brothers, 1944.

Miller, Raymond W. *Our Debt to the Ancients*. Washington, D.C.: New Age Magazine, 1974.

Moldenke, Harold N., and Moldenke, Alma L. *Plants of the Bible*. Waltham, Massachusetts: Chronica Botanica Company, 1952.

Morrison. Margaret. *Cosmetics, The Substances Beneath the Form*. Washington, D.C. U.S. Department of Health, Education, and Welfare. H.E.W. Publication No. F.D.A. 78-5007, 1978.

National Geographic Society. *Everyday Life in Bible Lands*. Washington, D.C., 1968.

––––––. *Map, Lands of the Bible Today*. Washington, D.C., 1968.

Navarra, Fernand. *Noah's Ark: I Touched It*. Plainfield, New Jersey: Logos International, 1974.

Plummer, A. Perry. *Oldman Wormwood*. Utah Science. March, 1974.

Robinson, Herbert Spencer. *Myths and Legends of all Nations*. Garden City, New York: Garden City Books, 1960.

Rohde, Eleanor Sinclair. *Garden-Craft in the Bible*. Freeport, New York: Books for Libraries Press, Inc., 1967.

Rosengarten, Frederic Jr. *The Book of Spices*. Philadelphia: Livingston Publishing Co., 1969.

Stewart, Rhea Tally. *A Dam at Marib*. Aramco World Magazine. Houston, Texas. March/April, 1978.

The American Schools of Oriental Research. *The Biblical Archaeologist*. Cambridge, Massachusetts.

Thomas, D. W., Editor. *Archaeology and Old Testament Study*. Society for Old Testament Study, 1967.

Thompson, Anthony Todd. *Philosophy of Magic, Prodigies, and Apparent Miracles*. New York: Harper and Brothers, 1862.

Time Magazine. "The Oldest Mine" January 13, 1975.

————. "Earth's Creeping Deserts." September 12, 1977.

Unger, Merrill F. *Unger's Bible Dictionary*. Chicago: Moody Press, 1973.

United States Forest Service, U.S.D.A. *Forests and Forest Devastation in the Bible*. Publication M-5204. Washington, D.C.

Untermeyer, Louis. *Plants of the Bible*. New York: Golden Press, 1968.

Warshofsky, Fred. "Noah, The Flood, the Facts." Pleasantville, New York: *Reader's Digest*, September, 1977.

Wheeler, J. Talboys. *The Life and Travels of Herodotus*. New York: Harper and Brothers, 1856.

Whiston, William (translator). *The Life and Works of Flavius Josephus*. Philadelphia: The John C. Winston Co., 1928.

Woolley, Sir Leonard. *Digging up the Past*. London: Ernest Benn Limited, 1954.

Wright, G. Ernest. *Biblical Archaeology*. Philadelphia: The Westminster Press, 1962.

General Index

Scripture Index